W9-BSF-993

HERBS

A COUNTRY GARDEN COOKBOOK

By Rosalind Creasy and Carole Saville

Photography by Kathryn Kleinman

CollinsPublishersSanFrancisco

A Division of HarperCollins*Publishers*

For my mother, always full of enthusiasm and abundant love. —Carole Saville
For R. J. —Rosalind Creasy

First published in USA 1995 by Collins Publishers San Francisco
Copyright © 1995 by Collins Publishers San Francisco
Recipe and text copyright © 1995 Rosalind Creasy and Carol Saville
Photographs copyright © 1995 Kathryn Kleinman
Food Stylist: Stephanie Greenleigh
Floral and Prop Stylist: Michaele Thunen
Art Direction and Design: Jennifer Barry
Series Editor: Meesha Halm
Illustrations copyright © Maryjo Koch
Library of Congress Cataloging-in-Publication Data
Herbs: a country garden cookbook/by Rosalind Creasy and Carole Saville;
photography by Kathryn Kleinman.
p.   cm.
Includes index.
ISBN 0-00-255453-4
1. Cookery (Herbs)   2. Herbs.   3. Herb gardening.
I. Saville, Carole.   II. Title.
TX819.H4C74 1995
641.6'57—dc20   CIP 94-29992

All rights reserved, including the right of reproduction in whole
or in part or in any form.

Printed in China
1 3 5 7 9 10 8 6 4 2

Acknowledgments

My many thanks for recipe ideas and testing, and much tasting, go to Gudi Riter, Julie Creasy, Dayna Lane, Jody Main, Helen Chan and Robert Creasy. Thanks as well to Carole Saville, herb maven and certainly the most influential person in my joyous herb adventure. —Rosalind Creasy

My thanks go to three men with excellent palates: my sons, Charley and Jason, and my husband, Brent. They devoured the recipes with curiosity and enthusiasm, giving educated culinary opinions and suggestions that I graciously accepted, because I respect their taste. My thanks also go to coauthor Rosalind Creasy, who is as much of a delight to work with professionally as she is as a personal friend. And to talented editor Meesha Halm goes the credit for tying the package together so nicely. —Carole Saville

Collins and the photography team would also like to thank Terry Greene, photo assistant; Cachet Bean, photo production; Patricia Brill and Rhonda Hildebrand, food styling assistants; Kristen Wurz, design and production coordinator; Jonathan Mills, production manager; and Assumpta Curry, production. Also to Ray Giacopazzi of Hillcrest Gardens in Petaluma; Susan Hastings; Hans Nehame; Delmy Rivera; Ed Haverty; and Michael Schwab for their props. And a special thanks to Thomas Keller at the French Laundry in Yountville, California.

H E R B S

A COUNTRY GARDEN COOKBOOK

CONTENTS

INTRODUCTION

Each spring brings the chorus of returning birds, the buzz of bees hard at work and the soft flush of new green leaves in a garden of herbs—all comforting signals that another growing season has arrived. The appearance of perennial herbs and the tender shoots of just-planted herb seedlings hold the promise of imparting fragrance and flavor to countless dishes. Then, when the mid-summer sun is high, the herb garden flourishes.

But an herb garden is generous with its gifts beyond the heat of summer. Chervil is in its prime in the cooler months. Dill seeds sown in spring can be planted once again in late summer for a new crop in the fall. Even in the winter, when herbs are at rest, they are still giving, for their bright flavors have been preserved in oils, jams and dried herbal blends.

The whole range of gardening passions, from the ornamental to the culinary, are satisfied by herb garden-ing. The herbs in the perennial bed reward your care by growing bigger each year. Annual herbs delight you in midsummer with their attractive and exuberant growth, with some even reseeding themselves the next year to save you the trouble. Tucked into the vegetable bed herb plants stand alongside the foods with which they are destined to be partnered in the kitchen.

Herb gardening is linked to a culinary history rich in both legend and practicality. Many of the herbs grown in contemporary gardens have been planted since ancient times and are being used today to flavor foods in much the same manner they were used in the past. The first-century Roman gourmand Apicius mixed parsley, rosemary, sage, mint and basil with garlic, olive oil and vinegar in a condiment he called "hot fish pickle" that was reminiscent of a vinaigrette. The sweet basil that is made into pesto at your local Italian restaurant is the same clove-scented herb used to flavor a *sauce verte* set out on medieval tables. Coriander seeds were used as an aphrodisiac in medieval love potions to bolster the waning interest of an adored one. Coriander seeds were even found in the tomb of Tutankhamen, leaving us to wonder just what plans the Egyptian king had for the herb in the afterlife. Another familiar herb, savory, derived from the Latin *satur,* meaning full, was considered in the late fifteenth century an herb of abundance and satiety as well as one that aroused passions.

More recently, in Early American kitchens, chamomile was used in tea, and rosemary, mint, thyme and bay were routinely used in cooking and as ingredients in natural insecticides. Savvy housewives also kept a well-tended bush of rosemary to take advantage of the adage, "Where rosemary flourishes, the woman rules."

A question pondered by every new generation of cooks and gardeners is, What is an herb? We are two gardeners long-involved with growing herbs in their many forms: annual, perennial, flowering, bulb, shrub and tree. In our opinion, an herb is a plant that is useful for its taste, its scent and its medicinal virtues. A second question commonly

follows: What is the difference between an herb and a spice? We like the definition that herbs are plants grown in temperate regions of the globe, while spices are grown in the tropics. A more specific distinction describes culinary herbs as a nonwoody plant's leaves, stems and flowers, and spices as a woody plant's seeds, roots, bark, fruit and buds. By the latter definition, however, some plants offer both herbs and spices. Dill, caraway, fennel, mustard, anise and cilantro all contain edible seeds that are generally considered spices.

In the end, the distinctions between herbs and spices are less important than the culinary treasures these remarkable plants hold. The simple act of making your way through the herb garden to pluck a sprig of this or a bouquet of that stimulates the imagination to choose the ideal herbs for whatever foods you are preparing. There are delicate herbs to flavor a fillet of fish and assertive herbs to flavor a fillet of venison. From gently perfumed chervil, parsley, lemon thyme and mint to robust rosemary, oregano, cilantro and sage, there is a flavor for every culinary occasion.

Even if you do not have a garden plot, you can still have the pleasure of cooking with herbs. A windowsill garden for apartment dwellers, a community garden on the roof or in a nearby empty lot, a container herb garden on the patio or a few herbs tucked in among the foundation plantings are all possible in the city or suburbs. And if you do not have a single spot of quality light in which a few herb plants can flourish, there is usually a city farmers' market where specialty farmers have done the cultivating for you.

The key to cooking with herbs is to infuse foods with just a suspicion of herbal flavor, to give foods complexity and

body but not to dominate them. A cook puts his or her own stamp on a dish by selecting the best herb or herbs to complement its main element. The recipes in this book call for certain herbs that are our personal choices, but our suggestions are just that. There is room to explore when cooking with herbs, so if you become partial to certain herbs or are curious about others, by all means substitute, mix and match and experiment. Such improvisation is part of the pleasure of cooking with these fragrant plants. Herbs offer the cook an opportunity to be creative, to break the routine of daily meal preparation. Cooking becomes more of a pleasure, a welcome challenge, and less of a chore. And the fragrant and flavorful dishes that you fashion will make you cherish your herb garden for both its beauty and its bounty.

GLOSSARY

Availability: Fresh garden herbs are obtainable at various times of the year, depending on the herb. Annual and biennial herbs have the most limited availability. For example, in the spring, parsley, cilantro and chervil are at their best, while summertime brings the glory days of basil and summer savory. Such perennials as tarragon, chives, thyme, sweet marjoram, oregano, mint, bay, rosemary, lavender and winter savory naturally flourish for longer periods. Gardeners in mild climates are able to harvest all but garlic chives and tarragon year-round, while northern gardeners can enjoy most of these same herbs only from May through October.

In the market, the seasons are blurred, as greenhouse growing and worldwide shipping put many herbs on store shelves throughout the year. As a general rule, however, if an herb is in season, it will be of higher quality and lower cost.

Gathering: The first rule of gathering herbs is to identify your herb accurately. Not all the plants in your garden are edible. We have provided Latin names in the growing section to help you make sure you have the correct plant. If you have any questions about which plant is which, ask at a nursery.

Choosing what to gather from the garden varies from plant to plant and from season to season. When you need only a sprig or two, and the plant is large enough to withstand the loss of a few leaves, snip a few inches from the end of a branch at any time of the day. This will also encourage bushy growth. Large, healthy plants can tolerate a sizable harvest; young or spindly, weak plants can abide only limited clipping. When cutting herbs to use fresh, cut them just before you need them and then wash them immediately to remove dust and critters.

When purchasing fresh herbs, choose a bunch that looks fresh, without any signs of wilting or yellowing. Don't worry if the best-looking bunch is too large for your needs; you can dry the remaining sprigs or use them to make flavored vinegars.

Storing: Storing methods for fresh herbs vary according to the type of herb. Basil is a warm-climate plant, for example, and should never be kept in the refrigerator. Instead, stand it in a glass of water placed in a sunny window, where it will stay fresh for days. Keep water level filled to the top of the container. In contrast, stand cooler-climate herbs, such as dill or cilantro, in water and refrigerate. In both cases, change the water once a week to prolong the life of the herb. Sturdier herbs, such as chives, mint, oregano, marjoram, parsley, rosemary, sage, tarragon and thyme, will stay fresh for a week or two if wrapped in damp paper towels, put in a sealed plastic bag and refrigerated.

Some herbs, such as basil, tarragon, mint, dill, fennel, chervil and chives, can be frozen successfully. Remove the leaves from the stems and discard the stems. Wash the leaves and blot or spin dry in a salad spinner. Put the leaves in lock-top freezer bags, close securely, label with herb name and date and freeze. They will keep well for up to 6 months; break off pieces of the frozen clusters as you need them. Once frozen, the herbs will lose their texture but retain their flavor. To use, chop the frozen herbs and add to soups, sauces and vinaigrettes.

Dried Herbs: There are times when running to the garden or market is inconvenient—when your herb plants are under a blanket of snow or your guests are about to arrive—so a cache of bright green dried herbs on the kitchen shelf is invaluable. Rosemary, sweet marjoram, sage, dill, savory, chamomile, lavender, thyme and oregano all dry well, while parsley, basil, chives, tarragon, chervil and cilantro generally do not. Even among the herbs that can be dried successfully, some fare better than others. The oils in oregano, for example, become concentrated, so the herb's rich flavor pleasantly intensifies. Rosemary also holds up well when dried, but because of its pungency, it must be used judiciously.

If you want to have certain classic herb blends on hand during the winter, it is necessary to dry even those herbs that lose much of their luster in the process. Among these herb combinations are French *fines herbes*—chervil, parsley, chives and tarragon in equal amounts—and the rustic mélange of dried thyme, summer savory, sweet marjoram, rosemary, bay laurel and lavender buds called *herbes de Provence*. Even the venerable French *bouquet garni* of bay laurel, thyme and parsley, tied together in a cheesecloth pouch for adding to stocks, soups or stews, may need to rely on dried herbs during the coldest months. Be sure to harvest these delicate herbs at their peak of growth to ensure that the fullest flavor possible is captured when they are dried.

How to Dry Herbs: Images of colonial homes with bouquets of drying herbs hanging from ceiling rafters may be picturesque, but there are less dusty ways to dry herbs. First, for any method used, quickly rinse the cut herbs and pat dry thoroughly or spin dry in a salad spinner.

To dry the herbs in a microwave oven, place them in a single layer between two sheets of paper towels in the microwave. Heat on high power in increments of 1 minute until the herbs are crisp and dry. Most herbs will dry in 3 to 4 minutes. Strip the dried leaves from the stems and place them whole in a small airtight jar. Label and store in a cool, dark place for no more than 1 year. At the end of that time, throw out any herbs that remain and start the process again.

To dry the herbs by hanging them, gather the cut herbs into a bundle, place stem end out in a brown paper bag and secure with a string. Suspend the bags, clothesline fashion, on a cord in a dry room or attic. Depending on the humidity, the herbs will be dry in 7 to 10 days. Strip the leaves from the stems and store as directed for microwave-dried herbs.

Herbs can be dried in the refrigerator as well. This method is best for drying small amounts of chopped herbs and can only be done in a frost-free refrigerator. Place chopped herbs on a plate on the refrigerator shelf, where they will be crisp and dry in 5 to 6 days. Whole stems will dry in a week. When crisp, transfer to glass jars and store as directed for microwave-dried herbs. They do not need to be refrigerated.

Cooking: Herbs can be added to foods in a myriad of forms, from fresh to dried, from whole sprigs to minced leaves. There are, however, a few guidelines to follow. In most dishes, use no more than one or two assertive herbs, although they may be mixed with subtler herbs. A few complementary combinations include sweet marjoram, thyme and oregano; dill, chives and parsley; basil, bay laurel and thyme; cilantro, sweet marjoram and chives; tarragon and parsley; and mint, parsley and chives. If you want to see how a combination of herbs will taste before you cook a dish, finely chop a small amount and mix into soft butter or cream cheese and spread on a cracker or piece of bread.

In general, use one-third the amount of dried herb to fresh for sweet marjoram, thyme or other subtle herbs. In other words, a recipe that lists 1 tablespoon of a fresh herb would use 1 teaspoon of that same herb dried. More pungent herbs, such as sage, rosemary and lavender, call for a different ratio. In these cases, one-sixth the amount of dried herb to fresh herb—1/2 teaspoon to 1 tablespoon—would usually be appropriate. Of course, there are times when you want a dish to "sing" of a singular sweet herb, such as mint, and you would then add a little more of it than usual.

Add herbs to a dish in small amounts, tasting as you go, until the flavor suits you. For long-cooking braised dishes, soups and stews, add the most pungent herbs at the beginning of cooking and the milder herbs when the dish is almost done. If you want the flavor of an herb, but do not want tiny specks of green in the dish, wrap the herb in several layers of cheesecloth, bring the corners together to form a pouch and tie securely with a loop of kitchen string to make it easy to retrieve. Before adding the pouch to the pot, wet it first by dipping it into cold water. This will help it to impart its flavor more readily. Herbs for *bouquet garni* can be placed in a mesh tea infuser, making it easy to remove.

To quickly remove herb leaves, hold the stem by the tip, right side up, and run your fingers down the stem against the growth. When using herb seeds such as dill or coriander in a vinaigrette, first soak the seeds in the vinegar for 15 minutes to soften them and release their flavor. A good way to unlock the flavor of dried herbs is to heat them briefly in a skillet; this releases their volatile oils for flavoring.

Collect twigs of rosemary, bay laurel (*not* California bay), oregano and sage, with leaves removed (save the leaves for drying), to throw on the grill, which imparts a delightful aroma to meats, poultry and vegetables when cooking out-doors. A natural basting brush to brush sauces on grilled foods as they cook can be fashioned from several lengths of thick rosemary leaves tied together, with the top leaves left on.

Throw complementary fresh herbs into the cooking water when boiling vegetables, then sprinkle with a handful of the same herb just before serving for an extra herbal punch. Dried herbs can be reconstituted in chicken or beef stock, wine or fortified wine, brandy or beer, depending upon the nature of the dish you are preparing.

An herb "salt" can be made from grinding together dried oregano, parsley and sweet marjoram, as they are all naturally high in sodium. And to perfume sugar for sprinkling over desserts or stirring into beverages, embed a sprig or two of lavender or mint in a covered sugar bowl.

To keep herbs looking fresh and firm for garnishes, cut herb sprigs early in the morning, and submerge their stems in water. Place in a cool area or refrigerate until serving time.

Basil: The traditional sweet basil has 2-inch-long, bright green leaves that grow on plants up to 2 1/2 feet tall. It has a spicy clove flavor with mint overtones and a distinctive perfume. Use the leaves whole or chopped. It is best used fresh, although it can be frozen with some success. It mates well with beef, eggs, cheese, white fish, onions, eggplant, beans, zucchini, mushrooms and tomatoes. Other basil varieties include lemon, purple, tiny-leafed Piccolo, cinnamon and Thai.

Bay Laurel: Bay laurel will grow as a tree to 40 feet, but can be kept pruned to a medium-sized shrub of 2 to 8 feet. The leaves, which have a resinous flavor fragrant with the scent of cloves, whether dried or fresh, are routinely added to a recipe whole and removed before serving. California bay *(Umbellularia californica)* should not be considered a substitute for bay laurel, as it contains toxic essential oils. Bay laurel is most often used in soups and stewed dishes filled with aromatic vegetables and meat or poultry.

Roman Chamomile and German Chamomile: Roman chamomile is a perennial ground cover with bright green, finely segmented foliage and white daisylike flowers. It forms a mat 2 to 6 inches high, but can mound to 12 inches. German chamomile is an annual that grows upright to 2 feet and has threadlike leaves and white daisylike flowers. Both plants have apple-scented blossoms, but German chamomile is less bitter and is the preferred flower for preparing tea.

Chervil: A delicate hardy annual with lacy, fernlike leaves, chervil resembles finely cut parsley with a mild anise taste. It grows to 2 feet, with white, umbrella-like flower clusters. Its subtle flavor is excellent in egg dishes, *beurre blanc,* cream sauces for fish, vinaigrettes, cream soups and in herb blends.

Chives and Garlic Chives: Common chive plants have delicate 8-inch-long grasslike leaves and round lavender flowers. Garlic chives, sometimes known as Chinese chives, have coarser flat leaves and white flowers. Use scissors to snip the blades into small pieces. The flowers are edible and should be used just as they open; if harvested when too mature, they will be dry and fibrous. Common chives, used fresh or dried, have a mild onion flavor that complements potatoes, carrots, cucumbers, egg dishes, pasta and green salads, soft cheeses, poultry and fish. Garlic chives have a pungent onion-garlic flavor that is particularly suited to Asian dishes.

Cilantro: Serrated, fernlike dark green leaves grow on plants that reach 3 feet. Cilantro's flat sprays of small white flowers are lovely added to salads. The seed heads are edible, too, and when mature are called coriander. Cilantro, sometimes referred to as fresh coriander or Chinese parsley, has a dark, earthy, intense flavor most people either love or hate. As it has little flavor when dried, it is most commonly used fresh to give a distinctive flavor to Mexican, Indian, Chinese and Thai dishes. Its unique character enhances tomatoes, onions, potatoes, salsas, curries, fish and shellfish.

Dill: This annual grows to 3 feet tall and 2 feet wide and has light green fernlike leaves with blue-green stems and flat yellow heads. Snip off young shoots and leaves and chop, use florets from flower heads for garnishing, and use seeds for flavoring vinegars or brines. Dill has a distinctive, aromatic, almost sour flavor that is perfect with carrots, beets, cucumbers, jicama, peas, spinach, beans, breads and pickles. It is also often used in egg, fish and lamb dishes and in salads.

English Lavender and French Lavender: English lavender is a perennial shrub that grows to about 3 feet and is gray-green to

Basil

Chamomile

Chervil

Bay Leaf

Lemon Balm

Mint

Sage

Savory

Sweet Marjoram

Cilantro

Chives

Dill

French Lavender

Oregano

Curly-Leaf Parsley

Italian Parsley

Tarragon

Thyme

Rosemary

silver. French lavender, which is also a perennial, grows to about the same size, and has toothed, fringed green or gray-green leaves. Both types have a lemon and floral flavor. Taste lavender before using, as some plants are not as mellow and rich as others; some even have a medicinal taste. Strip the leaves from the stems, chop finely and use in most fruit desserts, ice cream, and especially in lemon- and ginger-flavored dishes. The flower buds can be dried and used in *herbes de Provence.*

Lemon Balm: A citrus-scented perennial with pretty scalloped, heart-shaped, light green leaves that grow to 3 inches long. The plant, also known as Melissa, grows to about 2 feet. The leaves are best used fresh in hot and cold teas, wines, cordials, punches, jams and jellies, fruit desserts, salads, vegetables or whenever a delicate lemon scent is desirable.

Mint—Peppermint and Spearmint: Peppermint has a peppery taste and is best used in cooked dishes. It has toothed 2 1/2-inch-long leaves and grows to 3 feet. Spearmint is milder in flavor and is good in salads and other uncooked dishes. It has crinkly, pointed 2-inch-long leaves and grows to 3 feet. Both mints can be used interchangeably, depending on whether a strong or mild flavor is desired. Snip leaves from stems and use whole as a garnish or chopped for flavoring dishes. Use them for hot and cold drinks, for fish sauces, with lamb and chicken, in fruit and green salads, with carrots, potatoes and cucumbers and in desserts featuring fruit or chocolate.

Oregano: There is considerable confusion about which plant is the true culinary oregano. Greek oregano *(Origanum vulgare* subsp. *hirtum,* formerly known as *O. heracleoticum)* is a choice variety growing to 2 feet that most often blossoms white and has a penetratingly pungent scent. Rigani *(O. onites),* a harder-to-find but equally choice variety that is known as *pot marjoram,* has a peppery flavor and pale creamy white flowers. It has a smaller growth habit, up to 1 to 1 1/2 feet. Plants at the nursery simply labeled "oregano *(O. vulgare)*" are best left there, for the plant is musty and tasteless. The flavor of oregano is sometimes described as woodsy or resinous, and it is most commonly associated with Mediterranean cooking, particularly Italian, Turkish and Greek. Strip leaves from stems and use whole or chopped, or dry whole sprigs with leaves intact. Dried oregano, which is popularly used on pizzas and in tomato sauces, has a more intense flavor than fresh.

Curly-Leaf Parsley and Italian Parsley: Curly-leaf parsley grows to approximately 8 inches tall and the plants have a bright green, frilly appearance. Italian parsley grows to about 18 inches tall and has deep green, flat, celerylike leaves and a stronger flavor than its curly relative. Best used fresh, both varieties impart a rich, grassy and dusky flavor. Pick young leaves and use whole for a garnish or finely chopped for cooking. Italian parsley is considered the tastier of the two and is often used in Italian cooking mixed with oregano and thyme or rosemary or in Middle Eastern dishes.

Rosemary: Rosemary is a perennial with needlelike resinous leaves. It usually has small blue flowers, but certain varieties have pink or white blooms. Prostrate varieties grow 2 feet tall and 4 1/2 feet wide; others are erect and grow to 6 feet. Remove leaves, then chop finely before using. Fresh or dried, the taste of rosemary is described as piney and aromatic. Use in Italian and rustic French dishes, on pizzas and in bread doughs and with tomatoes, mushrooms, potatoes, eggplant, poultry, rabbit, lamb and soft cheeses.

Sage: A hardy perennial, sage is an upright, bushy, shrublike plant growing to 2 feet. Its gray-green leaves are used fresh or dried for their earthy flavor. There are numerous sage varieties with only a shadow of the distinctive sage flavor but with striking yellow or purple variegated leaves. Use sprigs of these showy sages for garnishes, but use the leaves from common sage whole or finely chopped for seasoning. Pair with pork, poultry, game, potatoes, beans, onions and cheese.

Winter Savory and Summer Savory: Winter savory is a creeping, deep green perennial herb growing to a little over 1 foot, and summer savory is a wispy warm-weather annual with reddish stems. Both have a spicy resinous flavor, although summer savory is milder and has a slight sweetness. Remove leaves from stems and chop finely before adding to recipes. Savory, fresh or dried, is an excellent addition to bean dishes.

Sweet Marjoram: This herb is closely related to oregano, hence its botanical name *(Origanum majorana),* but its scent and taste is pungently sweet as opposed to the hot and spicy taste of its relative. It is also known as *knotted marjoram,* due to its identifying swollen little buds or "knots" which form just before flowering with tiny white blossoms. Sweet marjoram is a shrubby, tender perennial growing to about 18 inches high. The heady, sweet scent of its velvety, gray-green leaves complements omelets, delicate soups, salad dressings, carrots, peppers, squashes and veal and chicken dishes.

Tarragon: A sprawling plant that grows to 2 feet tall, tarragon has long, slender leaves with a sweet anise flavor that are best used fresh. Tarragon flavors vinegars, mustards, vinaigrettes and sauces and is one of the four herbs used in *fines herbes.* Combine tarragon's licorice taste with eggs, poultry, fish, potatoes, cauliflower, lima beans, mushrooms and tomatoes.

Thyme and Lemon Thyme: There are hundreds of species of thyme, but *T. vulgaris,* or common thyme, is the one most recognized for its aroma and flavor. A shrubby perennial with upright growth and narrow, gray-green to dark green leaves, it grows to 1 foot high and equally as wide. Lemon thyme has the flavor of thyme with an added lemon overtone. Used fresh or dried, thyme leaves have a sweet aromatic flavor that makes this one of the most versatile of all herbs. Use only the tiny leaves; avoid using the woody stems. Thyme is a classic component of *herbes de Provence* and *bouquet garni.* The leaves, whole or chopped, complement eggs, pork, poultry, fish, veal, pasta, artichokes, potatoes, mushrooms, stuffings and stocks.

Growing Your Own Herbs: Herbs are arguably the easiest of all edible plants to grow. If planted in full sun in fast-draining soil, most herbs need little care except watering as needed and a spring pruning to keep them looking tidy. Pests and diseases are seldom an overwhelming problem, as the herbs' essential oils tend to discourage them naturally. In the Deep South, root diseases sometimes force gardeners to grow their herbs in containers. Herb plants of all types are usually started from plants purchased from a local nursery, from divisions from a friend's plants or from seeds. They can also be ordered by mail from specialty nurseries. The majority of gardeners find it easiest and fastest to buy transplants and set them out rather than starting them from seeds or cuttings. If you want to start your own herbs from cuttings, consult any comprehensive garden book and it will give you guidance.

Where to Grow Herbs: Herbs can be grown in their own garden, in a vegetable garden, interplanted in flower and shrub beds or in containers. With the exception of mint, chervil and parsley, most herbs require at least 6 hours of midday sun and good drainage. Chives, parsley, oregano, sweet marjoram, thyme, mint and parsley are also easily grown indoors on a sunny windowsill or warm porch. They all require bright light, a diluted dose of indoor plant food once a week and regular watering. If possible, give your indoor herbs a summer outside to rejuvenate them. Be sure to wash the foliage before bringing them inside to avoid introducing pest problems. Indoor herbs are occasionally prone to spider mites, mealy bugs, white flies and scale. The best defense is to keep them healthy with proper amounts of light, fertilizer and water. Outdoors, keep the garden free of weeds. If you have pest problems, consult your local nursery for suitable controls and make sure any recommendations are allowable on edible plants.

Planting Herbs: Dig a hole about twice the size of the plant's root ball in well-prepared soil. Place a little fertilizer and compost in the bottom of the hole and mix it in. Place the herb plant in the hole, cover the root ball with soil and gently push to settle the plant. Water the plant well and keep it well watered for the first month. After that, in rainy climates there will generally be enough moisture for perennial herbs.

Annual and shade-tolerant herbs such as parsley and mint will need to be kept fairly moist, however, and will require supplemental watering.

Once perennial herb plants are established, give them a fairly severe pruning in late spring to keep them bushy. In rainy climates, check soil occasionally and add water if the soil becomes dry between showers. The most drought-tolerant herbs are lavender, rosemary, oregano and sage, and in arid climates they can thrive with a twice-monthly watering. Fertilize your herbs in spring; if you have sandy soil, fertilize in midsummer as well. Annual herbs do best with a fertilizer application once a month.

Harvesting Herbs: Harvesting herbs is a delightfully aromatic job. When cutting them for drying, clip them when they are just about to blossom to maximize their fragrance and flavor. This is the point at which their essential oils are at their highest level. Mints are an exception to this rule and should be harvested when in full flower. Early on a dry warmweather morning, after the dew has left their leaves, but before the sun diminishes their volatile oils, is the best time to cut herbs for drying, as they depend solely on these volatile oils for the quality of their flavor and fragrance. Most herbs can be harvested more than once a season. They may be cut back by one-third during midseason when their growth is exuberant. In cold winter areas where it freezes, the last harvest of perennial herbs should be done no later than one month before the first frost so that the plant is not weakened and lost over the winter. Annual herbs may simply be pulled up or cut to the ground at the end of the growing season.

Basil (Ocimum basilicum): A hot-weather annual that grows poorly in cool coastal areas and tolerates no frost. Start basil from seeds or buy plants and plant them in full sun. Plant seeds 1/8 inch deep in warm, fertile, well-drained soil. Keep the soil moist while the seeds are germinating and the plants watered during the growing season. Watch for snails and slugs. Basil plants are exuberant growers; pinch back often during the growing season to encourage compact foliage. Grow 3 plants for seasoning and 6 or more for making pesto.

Bay Laurel (Laurus nobilis): A perennial that grows very slowly from seeds or cuttings, so it's best to purchase established plants of bay laurel. In the coldest winter areas, bay must winter indoors. As most cooks need but a few leaves, it is often grown as a potted plant, which grows to 5 feet. Bay prefers partial shade, especially in hot summer areas, where afternoon shade is a must. Fertilize regularly to encourage growth.

Roman Chamomile (Chamaemelum nobile) and German Chamomile (Matricaria recutita): Roman chamomile, a perennial, grows best in full sun in dry acid soil with good drainage. German chamomile, an annual, likes the same growing conditions and self-sows freely, ensuring a good supply of flowers for making tea. Both grow readily from seeds, and plants of the perennial Roman chamomile are generally available at nurseries in the spring.

Chervil (Anthriscus cerefolium): An annual that grows well both in the ground and as a container plant, chervil can be started from seed or nursery plants. Although its flavor is best in the cooler months of spring and fall, chervil can be sown every few weeks for a continuous supply throughout the growing season. Cut off developing flower heads to promote leaf production. Plant chervil in shade or filtered shade in rich, well-drained soil.

Chives (Allium schoenoprasum) and Garlic Chives (A. tuberosum): Hardy perennials that grow best in full sun. Obtain 2 or 3 plants from a friend or the nursery in spring or summer and plant in average, well-drained garden soil. Keep the soil fairly moist during the growing season. To keep plants looking tidy, cut them back occasionally. Harvest leaves, cutting them off at the base of the plant, anytime after the plants are a few inches wide. Divide clumps every 3 years.

Cilantro (Coriandrum sativum): This cool-season annual grows most readily from seeds. It is short-lived, however, and successive plantings in cool weather a few weeks apart are needed to ensure a steady harvest. In full sun, scatter seeds over a well-prepared 2-foot-square bed of organic soil and cover lightly with soil. Keep the bed evenly moist and start harvesting leaves when plants are 6 inches high. If plants are water-stressed or the weather is too hot, they will flower quickly and produce the edible seeds called coriander. One variety, Slobolt, is available from mail-order nurseries and goes to seed less readily than common cilantro.

Dill (Anethum graveolens): A tender annual that is short-lived in arid or hot climates, where it must be planted in both spring and fall. Sow seeds and grow as you would cilantro. Start harvesting leaves when the plants are about 6 inches high.

English Lavender (Lavandula angustifolia) and French Lavender (L. dentata): Although both perennials, English lavender and French lavender are treated differently in cold climates. English lavender is winter hardy, but French lavender is more tender and should winter indoors in climates where temperatures drop to 20 degrees F. Both lavenders are evergreen in frost-free areas in warm-weather climates. Most lavender is difficult to grow from seed; however, two reliable, easy-to-grow English lavenders have been introduced in the past few years. Lavender "Munsted," Waller's strain, is a semidwarf heirloom variety, growing to 18 inches, which blooms in its second growing season. "Lady" lavender, which grows to 15 inches, is excellent for gardens with short growing seasons, for it flowers its first season from spring-sown seed.

Lemon Balm (Melissa officinalis): Also known as *melissa,* lemon balm is a hardy perennial that thrives in shade and moist conditions, but it will tolerate partial sun if kept well watered. It can be started from seeds or plants and can also be propagated by root division in late fall. It spreads but is not unmanageably invasive. Lemon balm dies back in winter and reappears the following spring.

Mint—Peppermint (Menta piperita) and Spearmint (Mentha spicata): A fairly hardy perennial that grows best in partial shade in moist, well-drained soil. Most gardeners start mint plants with shoots from friends' gardens or plants from a nursery. Mints form underground runners that spread rampantly. For control, cut the bottom out of a 5-gallon plastic nursery container, place the plant in the container and "plant" the container in the ground. Water mint regularly in arid climates, and prune throughout the season to control.

Oregano (Origanum sp): Hardy perennial grown from plants, cuttings or seeds. Greek oregano *(Origanum vulgare* subsp. *hirtum,* formerly known as *O. heracleoticum)* is excellent started from seed, while pot marjoram, also known as *rigani (O. onites),* does best from nursery plants or cuttings. Full sun and good drainage are requisite growing conditions for this Mediterranean herb. Allow room to spread, about 2 feet.

Parsley—Curly-Leaf Parsley (Petroselinum crispum var. crispum) and Italian Parsley (P. crispum var. neapolitanum): Start these biennials from seeds or plants. Grow parsley in full sun or partial shade in fertile, well-drained, moist soil. Scatter seeds over a well-prepared bed and cover lightly with soil. Keep soil moist and be patient; the seeds are notoriously slow to sprout. Watch for slugs. In hot-summer areas, parsley grows best in the spring or fall. Fertilize if foliage pales. Although both parsleys are biennials, they are commonly treated as annuals because the leaves lose their flavor when the flowers appear in the second year.

Rosemary (Rosmarinus officinalis): A tender perennial usually started from nursery plants. Rosemary grows best in full sun in ordinary soil that is extremely well drained. In general, rosemary is free of pests and diseases. Spider mites are an occasional problem in dry climates, and nematodes and root rot can turn up in the southern United States. Grow in containers in cold-winter areas so it can be brought inside in the fall. One plant is usually enough for most cooks' kitchen needs.

Sage (Salvia officinalis): A hardy perennial usually started from nursery plants. Plant in full sun in fast-draining soil. In arid climates, water twice a month. Normally, sage is not troubled by pests or diseases, but it can succumb to root rot with bad drainage. One plant is sufficient for most cooks' needs.

Savory—Winter Savory (Satureja montana) and Summer Savory (S. hortensis): Both are easy to grow. Perennial winter savory germinates slowly from seed and should be started indoors 3 or 4 months before planting, so it is more convenient to purchase small plants from the nursery. Place winter savory in the front of the garden bed, as it is a pretty edging with its glossy green leaves and mounding habit. Summer savory can be started indoors and germinates quickly, but it can also be seeded directly in the garden once the soil has warmed. Keep soil moist during the germination period. After the growing season, cut the entire plant for drying. Winter savory will still be there when the weather is cold.

Sweet Marjoram (Origanum majorana): A small, slow-growing perennial which grows to 18 inches. In cold areas it is usually grown as an annual and replanted every spring. Its soft, gray-green leaves are much greener in warm climates, where it is grown as a perennial. Start from seeds or with nursery plants. Grow in full sun in well-drained soil. Pinch the top of the plant to promote bushy growth.

Tarragon (Artemisia dracunculus var. sativa): Start this hardy perennial from nursery plants, root divisions or stem cuttings only, as the culinary tarragon, also known as French tarragon, does not set seed. Do not confuse it with Russian tarragon,

known botanically as simply *Artemisia dracunculus,* which is available in seed form. The best way to tell which plant you have is to taste it. Grow tarragon in well-drained soil in full sun. In cold climates, provide a winter mulch. In warm-winter areas, treat it as an annual and replant every spring.

Thyme—Thyme (Thymus vulgaris) and Lemon Thyme (T. citriodorus): Common and lemon thymes are hardy perennials available as plants in the nursery. They grow best in full sun in ordinary well-drained soil. In arid climates, water a few times a month. Prune old growth of established plants in spring, and cut back by about one-third in midsummer to keep the plant from getting too woody and untidy. In general, pests and diseases don't bother thyme, but the plants can succumb to root rot with bad drainage. Southern gardeners sometimes battle nematodes and plant thyme in containers to solve the problem. One plant of each type satisfies most cooks.

Seed and Plant Sources

Fox Hill Farm
434 West Michigan Avenue
Parma, Michigan 49269

Nichols Garden Nursery
1190 North Pacific Highway
Albany, Oregon 97321-4598

Richters
Goodwood, Ontario
LOC 1A0 Canada

Sandy Mush Herb Nursery
Route 2, Surrett Cove Road
Leicester, North Carolina 28748

Shepherd's Garden Seeds
Shipping Office
30 Irene Street
Torrington, Connecticut
06790

The Cook's Garden
P.O. Box 535
Londonderry, Vermont 05148

Well-Sweep Herb Farm
317 Mt. Bethel Road
Port Murray, New Jersey
07865

OPENERS

The opening course of any meal is intended to whet the appetite for the course or courses that follow. From warming soups to sprightly salads, herbs can be used in myriad ways to get the meal started.

No medieval "salat" worth its salt would be without its sweet herbs, bitter lettuces and edible flowers. The utterly contemporary Garden Fresh Mesclun, flecked with blossoms and rich with variety, is a variation on that historical opener.

For another classic combination, a tart vinaigrette perfumed with the pungent scent of winter savory dresses skinny French green beans in the Haricots Verts Salad with Winter Savory Vinaigrette. And the cool, sweet flavors of the Jicama Salad with Spearmint and Honey Dressing is certain to alert even the most reticent appetite.

Even a cheese board can take part in opening ceremonies if the cheeses are light and delicate, with just enough bite to sharpen one's taste buds. A goat cheese dip mixed with a "thousand herbs" and an artistic assortment of canapés spread with chive-flavored cream cheese and topped with a mélange of colorful herbs and edible flowers are two hors d'oeuvres guaranteed to stimulate the eyes as well as the palate.

Carrot Soup with Onion and Dill Cream

*The bright sweet flavors of the carrot soup contrast beautifully
with the dusky flavors of the onion and dill cream.*

1 cup half-and-half
Two 3-inch sprigs of fresh dill
Two 3-inch sprigs of fresh Italian parsley
4 cups coarsely chopped carrots
2 cups finely chopped yellow onions
2 tablespoons vegetable oil

1 clove garlic, coarsely chopped
*2 to 2 1/2 cups chicken stock, preferably
  homemade or canned low-sodium broth*
Salt and freshly ground black pepper, to taste
Sprigs of fresh dill or Italian parsley, for garnish

In a small saucepan, heat 3/4 cup of the half-and-half until small bubbles form along the edge of the pan. Add the 2 dill sprigs and the 2 parsley sprigs and immediately remove from the heat. Set aside to steep for approximately 30 minutes to allow the flavors to blend.

Place the carrots on a steamer rack over gently boiling water, cover and steam for 15 minutes, or until tender. Set aside.

In a small skillet over medium-low heat, sauté the onions in the oil for approximately 10 minutes, or until translucent. Add the garlic and sauté for another minute. Transfer the onion mixture to a food processor fitted with a metal blade or to a blender and purée until smooth. Remove 1/2 cup of the onion purée and set aside.

Add the steamed carrots to the onions remaining in the food processor and purée until smooth. Scrape the mixture into a medium saucepan. Stir in 2 cups of the chicken stock and simmer over medium heat for 1 minute. (The soup may be prepared up to this point and then covered and refrigerated for up to 1 day before continuing.) Stir in the remaining 1/4 cup half-and-half and heat to serving temperature. Season with salt and pepper. If the soup is too thick, add as much of the remaining 1/2 cup chicken stock as necessary to achieve the correct consistency. Keep warm, but do not allow to boil, or it may curdle.

Strain the reserved dill and parsley cream into a small saucepan and discard the herb sprigs. Place over low heat and stir in the reserved 1/2 cup puréed onions. Heat to serving temperature, but do not allow to boil, or it may curdle.

To serve, divide the soup evenly among 4 individual shallow soup bowls. Carefully ladle approximately 1/4 cup of the onion-cream mixture into the center of each dish. Place a sprig of dill or parsley onto the center of the onion-cream mixture and serve immediately.
Serves 4

Pork Dumpling Soup with Garlic Chives

This lovely soup works equally well with common chives in place of the garlic chives.

Dumplings:

1/3 pound lean ground pork
3/4 cup finely chopped green cabbage
1/2 cup finely grated carrot
1/2 cup finely chopped fresh garlic chives
2 tablespoons finely grated, peeled fresh ginger
1 tablespoon finely chopped fresh cilantro
1/2 teaspoon freshly ground black pepper
1 teaspoon Tabasco sauce (optional)
1 egg, lightly beaten

One 12-ounce package 3-inch-square wonton skins
*   (thawed, if frozen)*

Soup:

1 large head bok choy or large bunch spinach
8 cups vegetable or chicken stock, preferably
*   homemade or canned low-sodium broth*
2 tablespoons finely grated, peeled fresh ginger
10 to 12 mushrooms, thinly sliced
2 tablespoons finely chopped fresh garlic chives
Fresh cilantro leaves, for garnish

To make the dumplings, sauté the pork in a small skillet over medium heat for 5 minutes, or until browned. Place in a medium mixing bowl and let cool. Add the cabbage, carrot, chives, ginger, cilantro, black pepper and hot sauce (if using) and stir well. Add the egg and stir well.

Working with only 2 or 3 wonton skins at a time, set out the skins on a clean work surface or plate. Keep the others covered with a damp kitchen towel to prevent them from drying out. Place a rounded teaspoon of filling in the middle of each square. Dampen the top corner and one edge of the square with water, fold the bottom half over the filling to cover completely and form a triangle and press the edges together at the top to seal. Bring the two bottom corners around to meet, overlapping them slightly, and pinch to seal. The folded dumpling should resemble a nurse's cap. Place the finished dumplings on a baking sheet; do not allow them to touch. Cover with plastic wrap and refrigerate if not using immediately. (The dumplings also freeze beautifully. Freeze on baking sheets to prevent them from sticking together, then transfer the fully frozen dumplings to freezer bags and freeze for up to 2 months.)

To make the soup, cut the green leafy portions of the bok choy into narrow strips; reserve the large white stems for another use. If using spinach, discard the tough stems and slice the leaves into narrow strips.

Pour the stock into a large pot and add the ginger. Bring to a simmer over medium heat and add the mushrooms. Simmer for 1 minute. Add the bok choy or spinach, dumplings and chives to the simmering stock and cook for approximately 4 minutes, or until the dumplings become transparent.

To serve, ladle 6 or so dumplings into each individual large soup bowl. Ladle the soup over the dumplings and garnish with the cilantro.
Serves 6 to 8

Garden Fresh Mesclun

Mesclun is a French Provençal word for a salad mix that combines the many flavors and textures of greens and herbs. Harvest the greens, herbs and edible flowers from your garden or seek them out at a farmers' market or produce stand.

Approximately 6 handfuls of mixed salad greens, including baby lettuces and young leaves of spinach, mizuna, arugula, mâche, radicchio, sorrel and frisée, in any combination
Handful of mixed fresh herb leaves, including Italian parsley, chervil, spearmint and sweet basil leaves, in any combination

Shallot Vinaigrette:
1/4 cup balsamic vinegar
1 medium shallot, minced
Salt and freshly ground black pepper, to taste
6 tablespoons extra virgin olive oil

10 to 12 pesticide-free fresh edible flowers, such as nasturtiums, violas, borage blossoms or calendulas, for garnish (optional)

Wash greens and herbs carefully, then dry them in a salad spinner or lay them out on paper towels and gently blot them with more towels. Transfer to a large salad bowl. If not serving immediately, cover with plastic wrap and re-frigerate for up to 4 hours.

To make the vinaigrette, in a small bowl, whisk together the vinegar, shallot, salt and pepper. Whisk in the olive oil.

Gently rinse the flowers (if using) and pat dry with paper towels. Pour the vinaigrette over the greens and herbs and toss gently. Garnish with the flowers and serve at once. *Serves 6 to 8*

Veronique's Doucette with Fines Herbes and Honey Orange Dressing

French friend Veronique's oil-free dressing is a honey lover's delight for tossing with a spring salad of doucette, the delicate rosette lettuce more commonly known as mâche or lamb's lettuce.

4 handfuls of mâche leaves or butter lettuce leaves, or a combination, carefully washed and dried

Fines Herbes and Honey Orange Dressing:
1/2 cup freshly squeezed orange juice
2 tablespoons clover honey
Pinch of salt
Freshly ground white pepper, to taste
1 teaspoon finely chopped fresh chervil
1 teaspoon finely chopped fresh chives
1 teaspoon finely chopped fresh tarragon
1 teaspoon finely chopped fresh parsley

Toasted sliced hazelnuts, for garnish (optional)

Place the lettuce in a medium salad bowl. In a small bowl, whisk together all the ingredients for the dressing. Drizzle the dressing over the lettuce and toss gently.

Divide the salad among 4 plates. Scatter the hazelnuts over the top, if desired. Serve immediately. *Serves 4*

Artist's Palette Herb Flower Canapés

Feature your garden and your artistry with a tray of splashy hors d'oeuvres that are each one of a kind.
Almost all the culinary herbs are suitable for these lovely treats, so harvest a fanciful variety of sprigs and blossoms.
If you lack an herb garden, purchase a bunch each of Italian parsley, dill, thyme and basil. Edible flowers can be
sought out at your specialty produce market. (Avoid flowers from florist shops, as they are commonly sprayed with
chemicals not allowed on food.) Use rustic, dense loaves for the canapé bases; softer breads will not hold up.

1/2 pound natural cream cheese, at room temperature
3 tablespoons finely chopped fresh chives
3 to 5 tablespoons milk
2 large rectangular loaves firm, dense bread, unsliced

40 to 60 fresh herb flowers
20 to 30 fresh edible flowers
20 to 30 fresh herb sprigs

Place the cream cheese in a mixing bowl. Add the chives and 3 tablespoons of the milk and stir until smooth. If the mixture is too thick, add more of the milk as needed to thin to the correct consistency.

Using a serrated knife, trim the crusts from the loaves of bread. Cut the loaves into slices 1/3 inch thick. Cut each slice into 2 1/2- to 4-inch squares, 2-by-3-inch rectangles or 3-inch triangles. Spread the cream cheese mixture on the bread cutouts (use approximately 1 tablespoon per 2 1/2-inch square). Arrange the cutouts on baking sheets, cover with plastic wrap and refrigerate for up to 6 hours.

If possible, pick the herb flowers in the early morning when they are at their freshest. Choose from the flowers of both common and garlic chives, chamomile, chervil, cilantro, dill, oregano, rosemary, sage, sweet marjoram and thyme. If you have edible flowers, pick them as well. Select borage flowers, nasturtiums, pansies, violets and/or violas. (Caution: Be sure the flowers you pick are indeed edible, and that they have not been sprayed with pesticides unsuitable for edible plants.) Gently rinse all the flowers and stand them in water in the refrigerator for up to 6 hours.

Herb leaves are also useful for filling out the designs. Italian and curly-leaf parsleys, mint, dill, purple and sweet basils, sweet marjoram, oregano, thyme and the many variegated sages all work well. Carefully wash the leaves and gently pat them dry on paper towels. Lay them out on a baking sheet lined with damp paper towels and cover with plastic wrap. Refrigerate for up to 2 hours.

To assemble the canapés, decorate each cutout with an herb flower or an edible flower or two. Add a few contrasting herb leaves to each cutout. Use your imagination when mixing the different colors and textures. The hors d'oeuvre may be prepared a few hours in advance, covered with plastic wrap and refrigerated, but the less time before serving the fresher the flowers will be. To unify the design, put a paper doily on a decorative tray and transfer the hors d'oeuvres to the tray. Serve at once. *Serves 8 to 10*

Pear and Pecan Salad with Lemon Balm and Raspberry Vinaigrette

*Pears and toasted pecans complement each other. Add a raspberry vinaigrette
fragrant with the citrus oils of lemon balm to create a delicate fruit salad to whet the appetite.
Choose ripe Comice, Bartlett, Bosc or Anjou pears, depending on the season.*

Lemon Balm and Raspberry Vinaigrette:
1 tablespoon raspberry vinegar
1/4 teaspoon granulated sugar
Pinch of salt
Pinch of ground nutmeg
Freshly ground white pepper, to taste
*2 teaspoons finely chopped fresh lemon balm
   (or spearmint)*
3 tablespoons extra virgin olive oil

2 tablespoons pecans
*1 small head butter lettuce, leaves separated,
   carefully washed and dried*
*2 large ripe pears, peeled, quartered, cored and
   thinly sliced*
Sprigs of fresh lemon balm (or spearmint), for garnish

Preheat the oven to 375 degrees F.

Meanwhile, make the vinaigrette. In a small bowl, whisk together the vinegar, sugar, salt, nutmeg, pepper and lemon balm (or spearmint). Whisk in the olive oil. Set aside.

Spread the pecans in a small baking pan and toast in the oven for approximately 5 minutes, or until lightly browned. Let cool slightly and then chop coarsely.

Line 4 salad plates with the lettuce leaves. Arrange a sliced pear half atop the lettuce on each plate. Sprinkle the chopped pecans over the pears, then spoon the vinaigrette over the pears to coat lightly. Garnish with lemon balm (or spearmint) sprigs and serve at once. *Serves 4 to 6*

Goat Cheese with Mille Herbes

*The "thousand herbs" show off their combined
flavors in this tangy cheese dip. Serve it with a basket of
chilled crudités. Unthinned, it is delicious as a spread on
bite-sized crackers or as a base for a light sandwich.*

10 1/2 ounces fresh goat cheese, at room temperature
2 teaspoons finely minced fresh tarragon
2 teaspoons finely minced fresh Italian parsley
2 teaspoons finely minced fresh sweet marjoram
2 teaspoons finely minced fresh thyme
2 teaspoons finely minced fresh dill
2 teaspoons finely minced fresh sweet basil
1 teaspoon finely minced fresh chives
Pinch of cayenne pepper
Low-fat milk, for thinning

In a medium bowl, combine the cheese, herbs and
cayenne pepper. Stir until well blended. Add milk
to thin to the desired consistency.

Cover the bowl with plastic wrap and refrigerate for 1 hour to blend the flavors. Bring to room
temperature before serving. *Makes approximately
1 1/4 cups*

*Clockwise: Goat Cheese with Mille Herbs,
Haricots Verts Salad with Winter Savory
Vinaigrette (recipe p. 36) and Jicama Salad with
Spearmint and Honey Dressing (recipe p. 37)*

Haricots Verts Salad with Winter Savory Vinaigrette

The mating of winter savory and green beans is a classic pairing. Here, they come together in a simple salad that is easily assembled. Summer savory can be used in place of the winter savory; the taste will be more delicate.

Winter Savory Vinaigrette:
2 tablespoons freshly squeezed lemon juice
Salt and freshly ground black pepper, to taste
2 teaspoons Dijon mustard
1 tablespoon finely chopped shallots
1 clove garlic, minced

1 tablespoon finely chopped fresh winter savory
6 tablespoons extra virgin olive oil

1 tablespoon salt
1 1/4 pounds haricots verts or other young, tender
green beans, ends trimmed

To make the vinaigrette, in a medium bowl, whisk together the lemon juice, salt and pepper, mustard, shallots, garlic and winter savory. Whisk in the olive oil and set aside.

Select a bowl large enough to hold the green beans and fill it with ice water. Set aside. Bring a large saucepan of water to a boil and add the salt and beans. When the water returns to a boil, remove from the heat and drain the beans. Immediately rinse the beans under cold running water, then plunge them into the bowl of ice water. Allow to sit for 5 minutes, then drain thoroughly.

Pat the beans dry and place in a large bowl. Pour on the vinaigrette and toss to coat well. Divide among 4 chilled salad plates and serve immediately. *Serves 4*

Jicama Salad with Spearmint and Honey Dressing

*The sweet, crisp character of jicama is underscored by the honey dressing. Serve the salad cold to bring
out the cool, refreshing qualities of the mint and jicama. Lemon balm can be substituted for the spearmint
in the dressing and for lining the plate; increase the herb measure for the dressing to 2 tablespoons.*

*1 large jicama (approximately 1 1/2 pounds and
    5 to 6 inches across)*
*Fresh sprigs of spearmint, frilly lettuce leaves or white-
    and-green ornamental kale, for lining plate*

Spearmint and Honey Dressing:
Juice of 1 large lemon
1 tablespoon white wine vinegar

1/4 cup canola oil
1/2 teaspoon Dijon mustard
1 tablespoon honey
4 teaspoons finely chopped fresh spearmint
Salt, to taste
1/4 teaspoon freshly ground black pepper

2 medium tomatoes, sliced, or 12 cherry tomatoes

Using a small sharp knife, peel off the outer
brown skin from the jicama. Remove the thin
fibrous layer beneath the skin until you get
down to the firm white flesh. Slice the jicama
into thin rounds, then cut the rounds into
pencil-thick julienne strips.

Arrange a bed of spearmint sprigs or lettuce on a medium platter. Arrange the jicama
strips on the greens, leaving room for the tomatoes. Cover the platter with plastic wrap and
refrigerate for 30 minutes to chill the jicama.

To make the dressing, in a small bowl, whisk
together the lemon juice, vinegar, canola oil,
mustard, honey and spearmint. Whisk in the
salt and pepper.

Just before serving, finish decorating the
platter with the tomatoes. Whisk the dressing
once again to mix the ingredients, then drizzle
evenly over the vegetables. Serve at once.
Serves 4 to 6

ACCOMPANIMENTS

On a list of condiments for a ninth-century Roman household appear bay, sage, parsley, cilantro, mint, dill and marjoram. No doubt the cook plucked them fresh from the garden. Your own garden or a local produce market is still an ideal place to gather herbs to accompany foods as both flavorings and garnishes.

Vinegar is a universal accompaniment, and recipes for herb vinegars—flavored by thyme, tarragon, mint—are found in century-old American cookery books. In this chapter, we include a robust rosemary vinegar, which makes an excellent marinade for beef and lamb, and herbal brines to perk up green and black olives.

Butters, oils and marmalades capture and preserve the unique tastes of fresh herbs. Dried herbs, on the other hand, are ideal to perfume delicate honeys or can be mixed together in *herbes de Provence* and Italian herb blends for seasoning your own Mediterranean table.

Herbs tossed into the cooking water subtly permeate vegetables, such as the bay laurel leaves in Artichokes with Spearmint and Prosciutto Stuffing. And a spoonful of chopped fresh herbs folded into mashed potatoes at the last moment imparts a tantalizing fragrance.

Herb-Flavored Vinegars

A hot summer day when your culinary herbs are about to burst into flower is the best time to capture their aromatic oils. Bottling herbs in vinegar is a wonderful way to trap these flavors, and a pantry shelf of glistening bottles of red– or straw-colored vinegars is a rewarding sight.

Herb-flavored vinegars find their greatest use in salad dressings, mixed with oil or used alone. They are also excellent in marinades, sauces, pickling brines, and for bringing out the flavors of soups, fruits and cooked vegetables. A splash of herb vinegar in sparkling water makes an old-fashioned vinegar tonic contemporary.

Combine chives, dill, lavender, spearmint, lemon balm, sweet marjoram, tarragon, thyme and basil with white wine or unseasoned rice wine vinegars. The more assertive oregano, rosemary and sage marry well with red wine vinegar. Purple basils color white vinegar brilliant pink but impart only a mild flavor. Make basil vinegar with sweet basil for an intense flavor, and add purple basil for color. Other flavorings—garlic, onion, chili peppers—can be added to the vinegars. Do not heat the vinegar during preparation, as the acetic acid essential to preserving the herb flavor will be lost.

Vinegars must sit for a couple of weeks for the herbs to infuse them with flavor. And as pretty as the vinegars look in decorative bottles on a windowsill with the sun streaming through them, the light will quickly dissipate their flavor. Store your herbal treasures in a cool, dark place.

Tarragon Vinegar

The mild anise flavor of tarragon vinegar perfumes a vinaigrette ideal for a pear or orange salad or for sprinkling over sliced cucumbers. Or use it in place of lemon juice for a tarragon mayonnaise to dress a chicken salad.

2 cups fresh tarragon leaves and stems
1/3 cup sliced shallots
5 black peppercorns

2 cups white wine vinegar
Sprig of fresh tarragon (optional)

Rinse the tarragon leaves and stems and pat dry with paper towels. Place in a sterilized wide-mouthed 1-quart glass container with a nonreactive lid. Bruise the tarragon with a wooden pestle or the back of a wooden spoon. Add the shallots and peppercorns, then fill the jar with the vinegar, making sure the tarragon and other ingredients are submerged. Cover tightly and place in a cool, dark place for at least 2 weeks, or longer for a more intense flavor.

Strain through a paper coffee filter, cheesecloth or a fine-mesh sieve. Pour the strained vinegar through a clean plastic funnel into a sterilized 1-pint bottle with a nonreactive top. Add a sprig of tarragon, if desired, then cap and store for up to 1 year. *Makes 2 cups*

Rosemary Vinegar

This deep-flavored vinegar is excellent in beef marinades or coupled with garlic for dressing a cold lamb salad.
A tablespoon added to the cooking water delivers a pleasantly pungent edge to steamed artichokes.

2 cups fresh rosemary leaves and stems
4 cloves garlic, peeled

2 cups red wine vinegar
Sprig of fresh rosemary (optional)

Rinse the rosemary leaves and stems and pat dry with paper towels. Place in a sterilized wide-mouthed 1-quart glass container with a nonreactive lid. Bruise the rosemary with a wooden pestle or the back of a wooden spoon. Pierce the garlic cloves with a wooden skewer. Add them to the jar, then fill with the vinegar, making sure the rosemary is submerged. Cover tightly and place in a cool, dark place for 1 week, then remove the garlic.

Allow the rosemary to infuse for 1 more week, then strain the vinegar through a paper coffee filter, cheesecloth or a fine-mesh sieve. Pour the strained vinegar through a clean plastic funnel into a sterilized 1-pint bottle with a nonreactive top. Add a fresh sprig of rosemary, if desired, then cap and store for up to 1 year.
Makes 2 cups

Herb-Flavored Oils

Herb-flavored oils are wildly versatile. Use a fragrant rosemary oil for dipping crusty slices of Italian bread, a vinaigrette made with citrusy lemon thyme oil for perking up a green salad, or any one of a host of aromatic oils for drizzling over vegetables, rice dishes, soups and grilled seafood and meats.

Unlike herb vinegars, herb oils have a short life and must be refrigerated to prevent harmful bacteria and mold from forming. The key factors in the prevention of botulism are the acidity of the product, the amount of moisture in the herbs, and the temperature at which the product is stored. Therefore, we recommend acidifying the mixture by either spritzing the herbs first with an acid such as lemon juice or vinegar, or adding lemon juice directly to the mixture. The herbs are then steeped in the oil for a week, and then the infused oil is strained and returned to the refrigerator for up to 2 weeks.

If you have any questions about preserving, contact your local Cooperative Extension Service office.

Basil Oil

If you are a tomato lover, nothing beats a plate of fresh garden tomatoes
sprinkled with the minty, clovelike scent of basil oil, salt and freshly ground pepper.

2 cups firmly packed fresh sweet basil leaves
2 cups boiling water

2 teaspoons lemon juice
2 cups extra virgin olive oil

Place the basil leaves in a colander and rinse with cool water. Now pour the boiling water over the leaves. Allow to drain well, then pat thoroughly dry with paper towels.

In a food processor fitted with the metal blade, combine the basil with the lemon juice and 1/4 cup of the olive oil. Process to chop coarsely. With the motor running, pour in the remaining 1 3/4 cups oil in a thin, steady stream and process until the mixture is emulsified.

Transfer to a sterilized jar with a nonreactive lid and cover tightly. Refrigerate for 1 week.

Bring the oil to room temperature and strain through cheesecloth or a fine-mesh sieve. Return the strained oil to the same jar and then cover tightly. Store in the refrigerator for up to 2 weeks. (The oil will solidify and become cloudy, but will liquefy again after a few minutes at room temperature or if the jar is held briefly under hot water.) *Makes 1 1/2 to 2 cups*

Lemon Thyme Oil

*Trickle lemon thyme oil over a spinach salad or an avocado stuffed
with baby shrimp. It is also tasty and healthful used in place of butter on
cooked pearl onions, red and gold beets or Blue Lake green beans.*

*2 cups firmly packed fresh lemon thyme leaves
and stems*
2 cups boiling water

2 cups extra virgin olive oil
1 small lemon, washed, quartered and seeded
Juice of 1 lemon

Place the lemon thyme in a colander and rinse with cool water. Pour the boiling water over the thyme. Allow to drain well, then pat thoroughly dry with paper towels.

In a food processor fitted with the metal blade, combine the lemon thyme and 1/4 cup of the oil. Process to chop coarsely. With the motor running, pour in the remaining oil in a thin, steady stream and process until the mixture is emulsified. Transfer to a sterilized jar with a nonreactive lid. Add the quartered lemon and the lemon juice, then cover tightly. Refrigerate for 1 week.

Bring the oil to room temperature and strain through cheesecloth or a fine-mesh sieve. Return the strained oil to the same jar and cover tightly. Store in the refrigerator for up to 2 weeks. (The oil will solidify and become cloudy, but will liquefy again after a few minutes at room temperature or if the jar is held briefly under hot water.) *Makes 1 1/2 to 2 cups*

Italian Herb Blend

*This zesty dried herb blend combines
popular Italian herbs in a seasoning to enhance a
myriad of preparations, from pizzas, frittatas,
ravioli fillings and tomato sauces to grilled rabbit,
sautéed zucchini and braised artichokes.*

1 tablespoon dried oregano
1 tablespoon dried sweet marjoram
1 tablespoon dried chives
2 teaspoons dried rosemary
1 teaspoon dried fennel leaves
1 teaspoon dried sage
1 teaspoon dried mint

In a small bowl, combine all the ingredients.
Using the tips of your fingers, lightly crumble
the herbs. Stir together all the ingredients to
mix well. Pour into a glass jar and cover tightly.
Store in a cool, dark place for up to 1 year.
Makes approximately 1/3 cup

Note: See page 11 for directions on how to dry herbs.

Herbes de Provence

*While the rich soil of Provence gives imported
herbes de Provence a flavor particular to that region,
an inexpensive and tasty version can be made
from herbs grown in your garden or purchased at
the market and then dried. Use this blend in
salad dressings and for lamb and pork.*

1 tablespoon dried thyme leaves
1 tablespoon dried sweet marjoram leaves
1 tablespoon dried summer or winter savory leaves
1 tablespoon dried rosemary leaves
2 dried bay laurel leaves, finely crushed in a mortar
   or spice grinder
1 teaspoon dried lavender buds
1 teaspoon fennel seeds
2 teaspoons grated and dried orange zest

In a small bowl, place the thyme, sweet marjoram, savory and rosemary leaves. Using the
tips of your fingers, lightly crumble the leaves.
Add the crushed bay, lavender buds, fennel
seeds and orange zest. Stir together all the
ingredients to mix well.

Pour into a glass jar and cover tightly.
Store in a cool, dark place for up to 1 year.
Makes approximately 1/3 cup

Herb Honeys

Honey gives food a special bouquet, and the pairing of the nectar of bees with aromatic herbs is a natural. Dried sage, rosemary, thyme and *herbes de Provence* make appetizing honeys for savory dishes, while mint, lavender and chamomile honeys are perfect in sweet preparations and for flavoring black teas. Choose mild honeys that will best showcase the fragrance of the herbs. Use only dried herbs to infuse honey; fresh herbs can raise the moisture content of the honey, causing molds and spoilage.

Mediterranean Herb Honey

One 12-ounce jar clover or alfalfa honey
4 teaspoons herbes de Provence (recipe p.44),
crumbled

Remove the cap and foil covering from the honey jar. Place the *uncapped* jar in a saucepan with 2 inches of water. Bring the water to a simmer and warm the honey for 5 minutes.

Remove the jar from the water and immediately add the herbs. Cover tightly, then shake the jar to distribute the herbs evenly. Place the jar in a sunny window or a warm spot for up to 1 week to allow the flavors to blend.

When the flavor suits you, warm the honey as before to liquefy, then strain. Discard the herbs and immediately return the strained honey to the jar. Cover tightly and store at room temperature on a dark shelf for up to 6 months. If crystals form, simply warm the honey again as directed before using. This honey is excellent drizzled over strawberries or cherries and equally good as a glaze on roast leg of lamb. *Makes 1 1/2 cups*

Garden Sage Honey

One 12-ounce jar clover or alfalfa honey
4 teaspoons dried sage leaves, crumbled

Remove the cap and foil covering from the honey jar. Place the *uncapped* jar in a saucepan with 2 inches of water. Bring the water to a simmer and warm the honey for 5 minutes.

Remove the jar from the water and immediately add the sage. Cover tightly, then shake the jar to distribute the sage evenly. Place the jar in a sunny window or a warm spot for up to 1 week to allow the flavors to blend.

When the flavor suits you, warm the honey as before to liquefy, then strain. Discard the sage and immediately return the strained honey to the jar. Cover tightly and store at room temperature on a dark shelf for up to 6 months. If crystals form, simply warm the honey again as directed before using. This honey makes a perfect dressing for a salad of apples and cheddar cheese. *Makes 1 1/2 cups*

Counterclockwise, from top: Mediterranean Herb Honey, Garden Sage Honey, and Lemon and Melissa Marmalade (recipe p. 49)

Lemon and Melissa Marmalade

The poetic-sounding melissa, which means "honey bee" in Greek, is more commonly known as lemon balm. It is esteemed for its honey-sweet, lemon-scented leaves, which attract beneficial bees that pollinate the herb garden. Here the leaves subtly flavor a tart-and-sweet lemon marmalade that is excellent on breakfast biscuits and tea scones or as a relish to accompany chicken, duck or other feathered game. The recipe provides enough for a few extra jars for gift-giving. You'll find you can't keep it in stock.

3 pounds large, thin-skinned lemons, preferably Meyer
3 quarts water

3 pounds granulated sugar
1/4 cup finely minced melissa

Day 1: Wash the lemons, then cut into thin slices. Using the tip of a knife, dislodge the seeds from the slices onto a square of cheesecloth. Bring the corners of the cheesecloth together and tie securely with kitchen string.

Place the lemon slices and cheesecloth bag in a large ceramic bowl and add 1 1/2 quarts of the water. Cover with a clean dish towel and let stand at room temperature for 24 hours.

Day 2: Transfer the contents of the bowl to a large, nonreactive pot. Bring to a boil, then remove from the heat. Return the contents of the pot to the bowl and let stand until the lemons are cool. Re-cover the bowl with a clean dish towel and let stand for another 24 hours.

Day 3: Drain the lemons and cheesecloth bag, discarding the liquid. Return the lemons and the bag to the large, nonreactive pot. Add the remaining 1 1/2 quarts water. Place over medium heat and bring to a simmer. Cook for

approximately 30 minutes, or until a toothpick easily pierces the skin of the lemon slices.

Remove from heat and strain, reserving the liquid. Set the lemons aside. Pour the juice back into the pot and add the cheesecloth bag and the sugar. Bring to a boil, stirring to dissolve the sugar, and then reduce heat to medium. Simmer, uncovered, for approximately 30 minutes, or until the mixture becomes syrupy. Add reserved lemons to syrup and cook for 30 to 40 minutes, or until the mixture has thickened and coats the back of a spoon. Remove the cheesecloth bag and discard. Stir in the melissa and remove from the heat.

Spoon marmalade into hot, sterilized canning jars to within 1/8-inch of the rim and tightly seal with sterilized canning lids. Store in the refrigerator for up to 2 weeks. For longer shelf life, consult an authoritative source for the method of processing the marmalade in a water bath. *Makes 8 1/2 pints*

Fresh Tomato Salsa with Cilantro

*Here is one of numerous variations on
the salsa cruda that good cooks have been whipping
up for generations. You can finely chop the
ingredients by hand or in a food processor. If you use
the latter, be careful not to overchop, or the coarse
texture of the salsa will be lost.*

*2 to 3 fresh jalapeño chili peppers, finely chopped
4 green onions, including tender green tops,
    finely chopped
2 cloves garlic, finely chopped
4 large ripe tomatoes, finely chopped
1/4 cup finely chopped fresh cilantro
1 1/2 tablespoons freshly squeezed lemon juice
1/8 to 1/4 teaspoon salt*

In a bowl, stir together the chili peppers,
onions, garlic, tomatoes and cilantro. Add the
lemon juice and salt and stir to mix.

Serve at once. Any leftover salsa can be
brought to a simmer in a saucepan, cooled and
then stored tightly covered in the refrigerator
for up to 1 week. *Makes approximately 2 cups*

Pineapple and Papaya Salsa with Sweet Marjoram

*Sweet marjoram lends a dulcet herbal undertone
to this salsa. For a sweet and spicy flavor,
use sweet basil in its place. Serve this sprightly
concoction with grilled fish or meats.*

*3 cups fresh pineapple chunks
1 ripe papaya, halved, seeded and peeled
1 teaspoon brown sugar
1 teaspoon salt
1/4 cup finely chopped fresh sweet marjoram
1 tablespoon finely chopped green onion tops
1 1/2 teaspoons finely chopped fresh red chili pepper
1 tablespoon finely minced red bell pepper*

Place the pineapple in a food processor fitted
with the metal blade and process for 3 or 4
seconds, or until a coarse purée is formed.
Transfer to a medium bowl. Purée the papaya
in the same manner and transfer it to the bowl
holding the pineapple.

Add the brown sugar and salt to the fruits
and stir with a wooden spoon until they are
dissolved. Add the sweet marjoram, green
onion and chili pepper and stir to combine.

Blot the bell pepper between folded paper
towels to absorb any extra moisture, then stir
into the fruit mixture. Let stand at room temperature for 30 minutes to allow the flavors to
blend. *Makes approximately 4 cups*

Marinated Black Olives with Oregano and Parsley

This method for dressing up ripe olives gives olive lovers a good reason for buying the canned variety.

Brine:
2 cups water
2 tablespoons sea salt

1 large clove garlic, quartered lengthwise
One 6-ounce can pitted black olives, drained
1 tablespoon dried oregano, crumbled
1 teaspoon grated lemon zest
Juice of 1 lemon
1/4 cup white wine vinegar
Extra virgin olive oil
1 tablespoon finely chopped fresh Italian parsley

To make the brine, in a small saucepan, bring the water to a boil. Add the sea salt and stir until it is dissolved. Remove from the heat and let cool.

Meanwhile, crush each garlic quarter with the flat side of a chef's knife. Place the garlic in a sterilized wide-mouthed 3-cup glass jar with a nonreactive lid. Add the olives, oregano, lemon zest, lemon juice and vinegar. Cover the jar and shake it well to blend ingredients. Uncover, add the cooled brine, re-cover and shake again. Uncover and pour in enough olive oil to cover the surface with a layer 1/2 inch deep. Cover tightly and refrigerate for 1 week.

Before serving, bring the olives to room temperature. Using a slotted spoon, transfer the olives to a bowl. Add the parsley and toss to mix. Place the olives in a decorative serving bowl or use for a garnish. The olives can be stored in the refrigerator for up to 1 month. *Makes approximately 2 cups*

Marinated Green Olives with Tarragon and Bay

Herbs make canned green olives a special treat when served as hors d'oeuvres or as a piquant garnish.

Brine:
2 cups water
2 tablespoons sea salt
1 tablespoon finely chopped fresh tarragon
1 fresh or dried bay leaf, broken or cut into 4 or 5 pieces
Grated zest of 1 orange
1 tablespoon coriander seeds

One 6-ounce can pitted green olives, drained
2 teaspoons red pepper flakes
Juice of 1 orange
1/4 cup white wine vinegar
Extra virgin olive oil

To make the brine, in a small saucepan, bring the water to a boil. Add the sea salt and stir until it is dissolved. Add the tarragon, bay leaf, orange zest and coriander seeds. Reduce the heat to low and simmer, uncovered, for 3 to 5 minutes. Remove from the heat, cover and let cool.

Meanwhile, place the olives in a sterilized wide-mouthed 3-cup glass jar with a nonreactive lid. Add the red pepper flakes, orange juice and vinegar. Cover the jar and shake it well to blend the ingredients. Uncover, add the cooled brine, re-cover and shake again. Then uncover and pour in enough olive oil to cover the surface with a layer 1/2 inch deep. Cover tightly and refrigerate for 1 week.

Before serving, bring to room temperature. They can be stored in the refrigerator for up to 1 month. *Makes approximately 2 cups*

Rosemary Focaccia

*Here, rosemary is used to flavor a traditional
Italian flat bread, but other herbs, both fresh and dried,
can be used, including sweet basil, tarragon, oregano,
chives and thyme. If you like, top the oil-brushed
bread with olives, garlic slices and/or pieces of oil-packed
sun-dried tomatoes before it goes in the oven.*

1/4 cup lukewarm water
1 package (1 tablespoon) active dry yeast
1 1/2 cups cool water
2 1/2 tablespoons extra virgin olive oil
1 1/2 teaspoons salt, plus salt for sprinkling on top
2 1/2 tablespoons finely chopped fresh rosemary
4 to 4 1/4 cups unbleached all-purpose flour

Pour the lukewarm water into the bowl of a heavy-
duty stationary mixer fitted with the paddle attachment. Sprinkle the yeast over the lukewarm water,
stir until dissolved and let stand for approximately
5 minutes, or until creamy. Add the cool water,
1 1/2 tablespoons of the olive oil, the 1 1/2 teaspoons salt, rosemary and 3 cups of the flour and beat
for approximately 2 minutes, or until the flour is
absorbed. Replace the paddle with the dough hook.
With the mixer set on low speed, knead in the
remaining 1 to 1 1/4 cups flour, approximately
1/2 cup at a time, adding only as much of the flour
as needed to form a workable dough. Knead for
approximately 10 minutes, or until smooth and
elastic. Gather the dough into a ball. *(Continued on
page 54.)*

*Left to right: Marinated Green Olives with Tarragon
and Bay (recipe p. 51), Marinated Black Olives with
Oregano and Parsley (recipe p.51), Herb Flower
Butter (recipe p. 55), and Rosemary Focaccia.*

Alternatively, to make the dough by hand, dissolve the yeast in the lukewarm water in a large mixing bowl. Then, using a wooden spoon, beat in 3 cups of the flour, oil, salt and rosemary until the dough pulls away from the sides of the bowl. Turn out the dough onto a lightly floured board and knead for approximately 20 minutes, working in enough of the remaining 1 to 1 1/4 cups flour until dough is elastic and not sticky. Gather into a ball.

Place the dough in an oiled bowl and turn the dough to coat with oil on all sides. Cover the bowl with plastic wrap or a clean dish towel and set in a warm place to rise for approximately 1 1/2 hours, or until doubled in bulk.

Punch down the dough and turn out onto a lightly floured board. Knead briefly, then divide in half. Oil two 9- or 10-inch pie pans. Using a floured rolling pin, roll out each dough half into a 9- or 10-inch round. Place a round in each prepared pan. Cover with clean towels and let rise for 30 minutes.

Using your fingertips, make a few indentations approximately 1/2 inch deep in the surface of each round. Cover the dough with lightly dampened kitchen towels and let rise for another 2 hours, or until doubled in bulk.

Thirty minutes before the dough has risen fully, preheat the oven to 400 degrees F. Just before baking, brush the surface of the rounds with the remaining 1 tablespoon olive oil and sprinkle lightly with salt.

Place the breads in the oven. For a crispy crust, spray the tops with a water mister every 3 minutes during the first 10 minutes of baking. Bake for 25 to 30 minutes total, or until golden brown. Immediately invert the breads onto cooling racks. *Makes two 9- or 10-inch rounds*

Parsley and Chive Butter

Although this recipe features parsley and chives, other fresh herbs—sweet basil, cilantro, dill, sweet marjoram, spearmint, rosemary, tarragon, thyme—would also be delicious whipped into softened butter. Such butters are wonderful spread on breakfast toast or sandwiches; swirled into a sauce for fish, meats or vegetables; or laid atop a bowl of soup or a piece of grilled meat or fish. Other flavorings, such as hot-pepper sauce, lemon zest, capers, garlic or shallots, can also be added.

2 tablespoons finely minced fresh Italian parsley
2 tablespoons finely minced fresh chives
1 cup (2 sticks) unsalted butter, at room temperature
2 teaspoons freshly squeezed lemon juice
2 teaspoons Dijon mustard
Salt, to taste

In a small bowl, combine the parsley, chives and butter. Using a wooden spoon, cream together until well blended. Add the lemon juice, mustard and salt and stir until thoroughly incorporated.

The butter can be covered and stored in the mixing bowl or, using a rubber spatula, transferred to smaller bowls for storage. It can also be refrigerated for 5 minutes to firm up slightly and then shaped into a log approximately 1 inch in diameter for easy slicing into discs. Store well wrapped in the refrigerator for 1 to 2 weeks or freeze for up to 3 months.
Makes 1 cup

Herb Flower Butter

These herb flowers mimic the flavor of their leaves, but the scent is much milder, resulting in a mellow butter ideal for serving on poached trout or grilled salmon.

1 cup mixed fresh dill, rosemary, chive and basil flowers and purple basil leaves
1 cup (2 sticks) unsalted butter, at room temperature
2 teaspoons lemon juice

Wash the flowers and basil leaves and dry gently with paper towels. Pull the petals off of the chive blossoms. With a sharp chef's knife, finely mince all the herb flowers, including petals, and the basil leaves. Place in a small bowl, add the butter and lemon juice and, using a wooden spoon, cream together until well blended.

The butter can be covered and stored in the mixing bowl or, using a rubber spatula, transferred to smaller bowls for storage. It can also be refrigerated for 5 minutes to firm up slightly and then shaped into a log approximately 1 inch in diameter for easy slicing into discs. Store well wrapped in the refrigerator for 1 to 2 weeks or freeze for up to 3 months.
Makes 1 cup

Mashed Potatoes with Herbs

*Chopped mixed herbs folded into mashed potatoes just before serving infuses them with a bouquet
of fresh flavors. Tarragon or rosemary would be a good addition to the list of herbs. Leftover mashed potatoes
can be formed into patties and sautéed in a little butter for the next morning's breakfast.*

*2 to 2 1/2 pounds Yukon Gold or russet-type
potatoes (approximately 4 large potatoes),
peeled and cut into quarters*
1 clove garlic
1/2 cup milk
1/3 cup heavy cream

4 tablespoons (1/2 stick) unsalted butter
Dash of freshly grated nutmeg
1 1/2 teaspoons finely chopped fresh chives
1 tablespoon finely chopped fresh parsley
1 1/2 teaspoons finely chopped fresh thyme
Salt and freshly ground black pepper, to taste

In a large saucepan, place the potatoes and garlic. Add water to cover and bring to a boil. Boil for 10 to 15 minutes, or until a knife pierces through to the center of a potato quarter with only slight resistance. Be careful not to overcook.

Meanwhile, in a small saucepan over medium heat, combine the milk and cream and heat until small bubbles form along the edge of the pan; do not allow to boil. (Alternatively, heat in a nonmetal pitcher in a microwave oven.) Add the butter and nutmeg and heat just until the butter is melted. Keep warm.

When the potatoes are ready, drain them, capturing the garlic clove as well. Pass them both through a ricer or food mill placed over a medium bowl, or place in a bowl and beat with an electric mixer fitted with the paddle attachment until smooth. (Do not overbeat, or the potatoes will lose their fluffiness.) Transfer the potatoes to a large saucepan and place over medium heat. Using a wooden spoon, slowly stir in the milk mixture until a creamy consistency is formed. Fold in the chives, parsley, thyme and salt and pepper. Transfer to a warmed serving dish and serve immediately. *Serves 4*

Tabbouleh

*Although this summer salad originated in the Middle East, it has been adopted
by generations of cooks around the world. Serve as an accompaniment to grilled lamb or beef
or as a light main course with pita bread or Rosemary Focaccia (recipe p.52) for lunch.*

1 cup bulgur wheat
1 cup boiling water
2 to 3 tomatoes, finely chopped
1 small cucumber, peeled and diced
1 cup minced fresh Italian parsley
1/3 cup minced fresh spearmint
1 small clove garlic, minced

1/2 cup finely chopped green onions, including
   tender green tops
1/3 cup freshly squeezed lemon juice
1/3 cup extra virgin olive oil
Salt and freshly ground black pepper, to taste
8 to 10 romaine lettuce leaves
1/4 pound French feta cheese, sliced
Black olives

Place the bulgur in a large bowl and pour the boiling water over the top. Cover and let stand for 1 hour, tossing gently after about 20 minutes. Drain off any water that has not been absorbed.

Add the tomatoes, cucumber, parsley, spearmint, garlic, green onions, lemon juice, olive oil and salt and pepper. Mix well but gently. Cover and refrigerate for at least 3 hours or for up to 6 hours.

Just before serving, gently stir the salad, taste and adjust the seasoning. Lay the lettuce leaves around the perimeter of a platter. Spoon the salad into a mound in the center of the platter. Garnish with the feta cheese and black olives. Diners can use the lettuce leaves to scoop up servings of the tabbouleh. *Serves 6 to 8*

Left to right: Tabbouleh and Artichokes with Spearmint and Prosciutto Stuffing (recipe p. 60)

Artichokes with Spearmint and Prosciutto Stuffing

*Large globular artichokes are ideal edible containers for holding
a mint-laced herbal stuffing. They make a tasty accompaniment for a light supper.*

2 quarts water
2 tablespoons freshly squeezed lemon juice
4 large artichokes

Spearmint and Prosciutto Stuffing:
1 1/2 cups fine dried bread crumbs
1/4 cup freshly grated Parmesan cheese
1/4 cup freshly grated Pecorino Romano cheese
3/4 cup coarsely chopped fresh spearmint

1/4 cup coarsely chopped fresh Italian parsley
2 cloves garlic, minced
1/4 pound prosciutto, finely chopped
Salt and freshly ground black pepper, to taste
2/3 cup extra virgin olive oil

1 dried bay laurel leaf
3/4 cup dry white wine or dry vermouth
1 orange, halved

Pour the water into a large bowl and add the lemon juice. Set aside. Working with 1 artichoke at a time, slice off the stem end to make a level base. Using kitchen scissors, cut off any tough or bruised outer leaves, then trim the thorny tips off of all the leaves. As each artichoke is trimmed, slip it into the lemon water to prevent it from discoloring.

To make the stuffing, in a medium bowl, stir together the bread crumbs, cheeses, spearmint, parsley, garlic, prosciutto, salt and pepper. Add the olive oil and stir to combine thoroughly.

In a large nonreactive pot, pour in water to a depth of approximately 3 inches and bring to a boil. Reduce the heat to low and add the bay leaf and 1/2 cup of the wine. Place the artichokes in the pan, stem ends down, cover and simmer for 15 minutes.

Using a slotted utensil or tongs, transfer the artichokes to a plate. Discard the cooking liquid, reserving the bay leaf. When the artichokes are cool enough to handle, gently pull apart the leaves at the center of each artichoke and, with a spoon or a grapefruit knife, scrape out and discard the fuzzy choke.

Fill the centers of each artichoke with approximately 1 cup of the stuffing. Return the artichokes, stem ends down, to the pan and add the reserved bay leaf. Pour in the remaining 1/4 cup of wine and enough water to immerse the bottom 1/4 inch of leaves. Cover, bring to a simmer and cook gently for approximately 1 hour, or until leaves are tender and easily pulled away from the center.

Carefully lift out the artichokes with a slotted utensil or tongs, draining well, and place on 4 warmed plates. Squeeze the orange halves evenly over the stuffing and between the leaves of each artichoke. Serve immediately. *Serves 4*

MAIN COURSES

The remembrance of a meal enjoyed in the past is sometimes triggered by a fragrant scent in the present—a scent no doubt released by the herbs used to flavor a dish. The affinity of certain herbs for particular foods has become traditional: rosemary with lamb, parsley with ham, cilantro with tacos, tarragon with poultry, sage with pork, dill with salmon, basil in a marinara sauce.

But it is fun to challenge tradition. Pork mates equally well with a bouquet of floral tones in Braised Pork Tenderloin with Herbes de Provence, while briny shrimp are wonderful cloaked with a sauce of cilantro and parsley. Who says that marinara sauce has to be red? Try Penne with Golden Marinara Sauce and Italian Herbs to know why it doesn't. Tomatoes, which usually love basil, are fickle and turn to rosemary in the Tricolor Tomato Tart. Lemon thyme and oregano slipped under the skin of a Cornish game hen before roasting replace the expected tarragon.

Yet some culinary traditions are meant to be respected. And a huge pot filled with Louisiana-style Herbs and Spices Crab Boil is unquestionably just such a tradition.

*Left to right: Penne with Golden Marinara
Sauce and Italian Herbs (recipe p. 64), Grilled
Rainbow Vegetables with Basil (recipe p. 67),
and Pasta with Sweet Basil Pesto (recipe p. 68).*

Penne with Golden Marinara Sauce and Italian Herbs

*This marinara sauce is in lively contrast to heavier long-cooked sauces, plus its
golden color is a lovely surprise. If you like, substitute 2 teaspoons minced fresh rosemary or tarragon
for the sweet basil. Serve the pasta with garlic bread and a cold vegetable salad.*

*12 to 14 medium Golden Mandarin Cross, Golden
Jubilee or other golden tomatoes (approximately
4 pounds)*
1 1/2 tablespoons extra virgin olive oil
2 cloves garlic, minced
1/4 cup finely chopped yellow onion
Salt and freshly ground black pepper, to taste

2 to 3 tablespoons chopped fresh sweet basil
*1 1/2 tablespoons finely chopped fresh thyme, or
2 teaspoons dried thyme, crumbled*
*1 tablespoon finely chopped fresh oregano, or
1 1/2 teaspoons dried oregano, crumbled*
1 pound dried penne
Freshly grated Parmesan cheese, for topping

Fill a large saucepan two-thirds full with water and bring to a boil. With a small knife, cut an x on the bottom end of the tomatoes. Slip the tomatoes, a few at a time, into the water for approximately 30 seconds, or until the skins begin to loosen. Using a slotted spoon, remove the tomatoes from the water and, when cool enough to handle, slip off the skins. Cut the tomatoes in half and remove the seeds by holding the halves over a sink, squeezing them gently and then easing the seeds out with a small spoon. Coarsely chop the tomatoes. (You should have 4 1/2 to 5 cups chopped tomatoes.)

In a medium saucepan over low heat, warm the olive oil. Add the garlic and onion and sauté for approximately 5 minutes, or until translucent. Add the tomatoes and simmer over low heat, stirring occasionally, for approximately 45 minutes, or until most of the liquid has evaporated. Add the salt and pepper, basil, thyme and oregano and simmer for 5 minutes longer to blend the flavors.

Bring a large pot of salted water to a boil. Add the pasta and cook for approximately 5 minutes, or until al dente; check the package directions for cooking time.

Drain the pasta and divide it evenly among 4 warmed plates or pasta bowls. Spoon one-fourth of the sauce over each mound of noodles. Sprinkle each serving with a generous amount of Parmesan cheese and serve immediately. *Serves 4*

Grilled Rainbow Vegetables with Basil

Summer vegetables are delicious grilled. The basil and garlic marinade used here gives them an extra boost of flavor. A mixture of minced fresh thyme, oregano and rosemary can be used in place of the basil. Accompany the vegetables with focaccia and a warm spinach salad with hard-cooked eggs.

1 cup extra virgin olive oil
2 cloves garlic, pressed
1/4 cup minced fresh sweet basil
2 medium lavender eggplants, sliced crosswise
    1/2 inch thick
2 small yellow zucchini

2 small green zucchini
4 small red onions
2 red bell peppers, halved lengthwise, seeded and
    deribbed
2 yellow bell peppers, halved lengthwise, seeded and
    deribbed

In a small bowl, whisk together the olive oil, garlic and basil and let stand for at least 2 hours or for up to 12 hours in the refrigerator.

Arrange eggplants, zucchini, onions and bell peppers on 1 or 2 baking sheets and brush the tops with the seasoned oil. Prepare a fire in a charcoal grill. When the coals have died down partially, spread them evenly in the grill pan.

Arrange the vegetables, oiled side down, on the grill rack. (Depending on the size of the rack, you may need to grill the vegetables in batches.) Brush the tops of the vegetables with oil and turn them over when the first side is just starting to brown. The cooking time will vary depending on the intensity of the heat, the distance of the rack from the coals and the density of the vegetables. If cooking over medium-hot coals, plan on approximately 4 minutes on the first side and 3 minutes on the second side. Watch carefully and cook only until just tender; overcooked vegetables will fall apart.

Transfer the vegetables to a warmed platter and serve immediately. *Serves 4*

Pasta with Sweet Basil Pesto

Classic basil pesto is irresistible over fettuccine. But don't be limited by tradition:
Create a delicious Southwest pesto made from cilantro, Parmesan cheese, peanut oil and peanuts
or an Asian pesto made from Thai basil, spearmint and sesame oil. Delectable pestos can also be created from
sweet marjoram, sage, thyme, oregano, dill or winter or summer savory. Parsley, too, makes
a wonderfully fragrant pesto, alone or partnered with any of the above herbs.

3 tablespoons walnut pieces
1 tablespoon pine nuts
1 tablespoon coarsely chopped garlic
1 teaspoon salt
Freshly ground black pepper, to taste
2 cups loosely packed fresh basil leaves, preferably
   Piccolo variety

3 tablespoons coarsely chopped fresh Italian parsley
1/2 cup extra virgin olive oil
1/2 cup freshly grated Parmesan cheese
2 tablespoons freshly grated Pecorino Romano cheese
1 pound dried fettuccine

Preheat the oven to 375 degrees F. Spread the walnuts and pine nuts in a small baking pan and toast in the oven for approximately 5 minutes, or until lightly browned. Let cool.

In a food processor fitted with the metal blade or in a blender, combine the toasted nuts, garlic and salt. Process until finely chopped. Add the basil, parsley and 2 tablespoons of the olive oil and process until well blended. Scrape down the sides of the container. In a thin stream, slowly add the remaining olive oil and process until a smooth purée is formed. Transfer the mixture to a medium bowl and, using a whisk, beat in the cheeses. Cover with plastic wrap, pressing it directly onto the surface of the pesto to prevent discoloration. Set aside.

Bring a large pot of salted water to a boil. Add the pasta and cook for approximately 5 minutes, or until al dente; check the package directions for cooking time. Just before the pasta is ready, stir 1 to 2 tablespoons of the cooking water into the pesto to thin it.

Drain the pasta and place it in a warmed serving bowl. Add the pesto and quickly toss to coat the pasta evenly. Divide among 4 warmed plates or pasta bowls. Serve at once. *Serves 4*

Note: To make larger amounts of pesto for storing, double or triple the recipe, and prepare the pesto without garlic, cheese or nuts, which can be added just before serving for a fresher flavor. Add 1 teaspoon lemon juice per each 2/3 cup of pesto and combine well. Spoon the pesto into sterilized glass jars with nonreactive lids. Cover with 1/2-inch olive oil and tightly seal. Store immediately in the refrigerator for up to two weeks or freeze for up to 6 months.

Hearty Minestrone with Rosemary Pesto

*Although this rosemary pesto is not a traditional pesto, it gives the finished soup
a richness and aroma that is truly exceptional. You can use 1/4 cup chopped fresh sweet basil
in place of the rosemary. Serve the soup with crusty bread and a salad.*

3 tablespoons extra virgin olive oil
1 large yellow onion, thinly sliced
One 1/4-pound slice prosciutto (1/4 inch thick),
    cut into julienne strips
1/4 pound fresh portobello or white mushrooms,
    thinly sliced
2 large carrots, sliced 1/4 inch thick
4 large Swiss chard leaves, cut into thin strips
1 small head green cabbage, cored and thinly sliced
2 medium zucchini, sliced 1/4 inch thick
12 fresh plum tomatoes (about 1 1/2 pounds), peeled,
    seeded and chopped, or one 14 1/2-ounce can
    plum tomatoes, chopped, with juices
10 cups (2 1/2 quarts) chicken stock, preferably
    homemade or canned low-sodium broth
Salt and freshly ground black pepper, to taste

Rosemary Pesto:
2 large cloves garlic
1/4 cup chopped fresh Italian parsley
Leaves from one 5-inch-long sprig of fresh rosemary
6 tablespoons freshly grated Parmesan cheese
1/2 dried red chili pepper

1 cup baby lima beans (fresh or frozen)
1 1/2 cups cooked kidney beans (fresh or canned,
    then drained)
1/4 pound dried wide pasta noodles, broken into
    3-inch lengths, or pasta shells
Freshly grated Parmesan cheese, for serving

In a large frying pan over low heat, warm 2 tablespoons of the olive oil. Add the onion and prosciutto and sauté for approximately 10 minutes, or until the onion is translucent. Remove from the heat and set aside.

In a large pot over medium heat, warm the remaining 1 tablespoon oil. Add the mushrooms and sauté for 2 to 3 minutes, or until they start to darken. If they begin to stick to the pan, add 1 tablespoon of water to draw out their juices. Add the sautéed onion and prosciutto, carrots, chard, cabbage, zucchini, tomatoes and stock. Stir well and bring to a boil. Reduce the heat to low, cover and simmer for approximately 1 1/4 hours, or until the flavors are fully blended. Season with salt and pepper. (At this point, the soup can be cooled and refrigerated for up to 3 days or frozen for up to 2 months.)

Meanwhile, make the rosemary pesto. In a mortar, combine the garlic, parsley, rosemary, cheese and chili. Pound with a pestle until a crumbly paste is formed. (A blender can be used for this step, but chop the rosemary leaves before adding them to the blender.)

Uncover the soup and add the lima beans. Simmer for 3 minutes. Add the kidney beans and the pasta and cook for 5 to 10 minutes, or until the pasta is tender. Stir in the rosemary pesto. Ladle the soup into individual bowls. Pass Parmesan cheese at the table. *Serves 6 to 8*

Tricolor Tomato Tart

This spectacular main course is most dramatic if prepared with homegrown tomatoes of different colors. Serve it as the centerpiece of a light lunch, accompanied with a salad of mesclun and a cream soup. Leftover marinade can be used as a base for a vinaigrette dressing for a salad of greens or pasta. You can substitute 1/4 cup finely chopped fresh sweet basil for any one of the fresh herbs used.

Filling:
3 or 4 tomatoes, preferably a mixture of red, golden
    and orange varieties, thinly sliced
1/2 cup virgin olive oil
1 clove garlic, minced
1 tablespoon finely chopped fresh rosemary
1 tablespoon finely chopped fresh sweet marjoram
    or oregano

2 tablespoons finely chopped fresh chives
Salt and freshly ground black pepper, to taste

1 cup fresh goat cheese or natural cream cheese,
    at room temperature
4 to 6 tablespoons heavy cream, as needed
1 prebaked and cooled 9-inch tart shell

To make the filling, place the tomato slices in a shallow bowl. In a small bowl, whisk together the olive oil, garlic, rosemary, sweet marjoram, 1 tablespoon of the chives and salt and pepper. Pour over the tomatoes. Marinate at room temperature for at least 1 hour or for up to 2 hours. Occasionally drench the tomatoes with the marinade by gently tipping the bowl back and forth. Do not stir the tomato slices, as they may break apart.

Place the cheese in a mixing bowl and, using a wooden spoon, whip until creamy and smooth. Add in a few tablespoons of cream if the mixture doesn't look spreadable. Stir in the remaining 1 tablespoon chives. Gently spread the cheese evenly over the prebaked and cooled tart shell.

Using a slotted utensil, remove the tomatoes to a plate and set aside for a few minutes. Then tilt the plate, draining the tomatoes well. Reserve 1/4 cup of the marinade. Arrange the tomato slices in a decorative circular pattern over the cheese layer. Cover and refrigerate for up to 2 hours.

Serve chilled. Just before serving, brush the reserved marinade over the tomatoes. *Serves 6*

Leg of Lamb with Rosemary and Mustard Glaze

A magnificent main course special enough for any occasion. Serve with pan-roasted potatoes and a lovely spring vegetable, such as asparagus or peas.

1/3 cup Dijon mustard
1 clove garlic, minced
4 teaspoons finely chopped fresh rosemary
1 1/2 tablespoons extra virgin olive oil
1 leg of lamb (approximately 5 to 6 pounds)

In a small bowl, using a small whisk, mix together the mustard, garlic and 3 teaspoons of the rosemary. While continuing to whisk, add the oil, a few drops at a time, until all of it is incorporated. Set aside.

Trim most of the outside layer of fat from the lamb, leaving only a thin layer covering the filament that encases the flesh. Pat the lamb dry. Place the lamb in a nonreactive container and brush the top, bottom and sides evenly with the mustard mixture. Sprinkle the top with the remaining 1 teaspoon rosemary. Cover and refrigerate for at least 4 hours or for up to 12 hours to allow the flavors of the mustard mixture to penetrate the flesh.

Preheat the oven to 350 degrees F. Place the lamb in a shallow roasting pan and roast for 1 1/2 to 2 hours, or until a meat thermometer inserted in the thickest part away from the bone registers 145 degrees F. for medium-rare.

Transfer to a warmed serving platter and let stand for a few minutes, then carve and serve. *Serves 5 or 6*

Italian Baked Beans with Sage and Savory

Here is a mellow and healthful alternative to traditional American baked beans made with sugar and salt pork. It is prepared more quickly, too, as the beans are not soaked overnight and the baking time is only a few hours instead of the whole day. Serve accompanied with crusty garlic bread and a radicchio salad. The beans can also be toted along on a picnic or served in smaller portions as a side dish to accompany Italian sausage, fish or poultry.

7 cups hot water
2 cups dried small white beans (approximately 1 pound)
1/2 cup finely chopped yellow onion
2 tablespoons fruity extra virgin olive oil
5 fresh sage leaves
1 1/2 teaspoons finely chopped fresh summer savory, or 1 teaspoon finely chopped fresh winter savory
1 large clove garlic, minced
2 teaspoons Dijon mustard
Salt and freshly ground black pepper, to taste
Paprika

In a 3-quart saucepan, bring 7 cups hot water to a boil. Add the beans, reduce the heat to very low, cover and simmer very gently for 1 to 1 1/2 hours, or until the beans are tender. (If the water level drops below the surface of the beans, add more hot water as needed to cover.) Test the beans for doneness after 45 minutes.

Preheat the oven to 325 degrees F. In a small skillet over low heat, gently sauté the onion in the olive oil for approximately 5

minutes, or until translucent. Remove from the heat and set aside.

Drain the beans in a colander placed over a bowl to capture the liquid. Pour the beans into a large bowl and add the sautéed onion, sage, savory, garlic and mustard. Stir to combine. Season with salt and pepper. Transfer the bean mixture to a 2-quart casserole or bean pot. Add enough of the reserved bean liquid to cover the beans by 1/4 inch. (Add hot water if there is not enough bean liquid.) Sprinkle the top with paprika.

Place in the oven and bake for 2 to 3 hours, or until most of the liquid is absorbed and the top starts to brown. When done, the beans should be moist, not soupy, and have an inch or so of liquid at the bottom of the pot.

Just before serving, remove and discard the sage leaves. Serve warm or at room temperature in individual bowls. *Serves 4 to 6*

Roasted Cornish Hens with Lemon Thyme and Oregano

A simple and elegant way to prepare Cornish game hens or other fowl is to place herbs under the breast skin so that the flavors of the herbs combine with the poultry juices to baste the flesh. The following recipe calls for lemon thyme, although sweet basil, tarragon or rosemary would be splendid, too. When using rosemary or tarragon, use approximately half the amount, as their flavors are stronger than either thyme or basil. Serve with Mashed Potatoes with Herbs (recipe p. 57) and baked acorn squash cooked alongside the birds.

4 Cornish game hens (1 to 1 1/2 pounds each)
Freshly ground black pepper, to taste
2 tablespoons unsalted butter, melted, plus melted
   unsalted butter for basting
8 teaspoons finely chopped fresh lemon thyme

1 teaspoon grated lemon zest
1 teaspoon dried oregano, crumbled
4 cloves garlic, minced
1 lemon, thinly sliced

Preheat the oven to 425 degrees F. Rinse the hens and pat dry. Sprinkle the cavity of each hen with pepper. Using your forefinger, very gently loosen the skin over each breast by working your finger between the skin and breast meat to create a pocket. Be careful not to tear the skin.

In a small bowl, mix together the 2 tablespoons melted butter, 4 teaspoons of the lemon thyme, the lemon zest, oregano and half of the garlic until a paste is formed. Using your fingers, spread approximately one-fourth of the herb paste under the skin of each hen.

Combine the remaining garlic and lemon thyme and fill the cavity of each hen with one-fourth of the mixture and a few lemon slices. Truss hens and place on a rack in a large shallow roasting pan. Baste with melted butter.

Place the hens in the oven and roast for 45 to 60 minutes, or until golden brown and a meat thermometer inserted in the thickest part of the thigh away from the bone registers 180 degrees F. Watch carefully to prevent overcooking.

Remove the hens from the oven and remove the trussing string or pins. Serve immediately. *Serves 4*

Braised Pork Tenderloin with Herbes de Provence

The flavor of sweet Provençal herbs permeates this dish of
succulent pork tenderloin. Serve with baked fennel and couscous.

1 large or 2 small pork tenderloins (2 pounds
    total weight)
Salt and freshly ground black pepper, to taste
2 tablespoons virgin olive oil
1 cup coarsely chopped yellow onion

1 1/2 cups dry white wine or dry vermouth
2 teaspoons herbes de Provence (recipe p. 44)
1 tablespoon heavy cream
1 tablespoon unsalted butter

Season the tenderloin lightly with salt and pepper. In a large skillet, heat 1 tablespoon of the olive oil over high heat. Add the tenderloin and brown on both sides for approximately 10 minutes to sear the outside and seal in the juices. Do not crowd the pan. If the whole tenderloin will not fit in the skillet easily, cut in half or into smaller pieces and brown in batches. Transfer to a warmed plate and reserve.

Add the remaining 1 tablespoon oil to the skillet over low heat and sauté the onion for 2 or 3 minutes, or until they begin to soften. Return the tenderloin to the skillet. Add the wine and *herbes de Provence* and bring to a boil over high heat. Cover, reduce the heat to low and cook for approximately 45 minutes, until the fillet is tender.

Transfer the tenderloin to a warmed plate and keep warm. Raise the heat to high and boil the remaining skillet juices, uncovered, until the wine is reduced by half. Reduce the heat to medium, stir in the cream and cook for 1 minute. Swirl in the butter and remove from the heat.

Cut the tenderloin on the diagonal into slices 1 inch thick and divide among 4 warmed plates. Spoon the warm sauce over the pork and serve immediately. *Serves 4*

Salmon on the Rocks with Dill and Shallot Butter

*Enclosing fish or meats in a crust of salt is a classic cooking method that
seals in juices. Here, the heat from a bed of salt cooks the salmon gently and evenly,
and the dill and shallot butter permeates the fish as it steams in its own juices.*

1 pound rock salt or kosher salt

Dill and Shallot Butter:
*4 tablespoons (1/2 stick) unsalted butter,
    at room temperature*
2 tablespoons finely minced shallots
1 tablespoon finely chopped fresh dill
1/2 teaspoon freshly squeezed lemon juice

Pinch of cayenne pepper
Sea salt, to taste

*1/2 salmon fillet, center-to-tail cut with skin intact
    (approximately 2 pounds)*
*4 lemon wedges and several sprigs of fresh dill or
    yellow dill flowers, for garnish*

Place the rock or kosher salt in a large cast-iron skillet and heat, uncovered, over medium-high heat for approximately 35 minutes, or until the salt feels hot to the touch.

Meanwhile, make the dill and shallot butter. In a medium bowl, using a wooden spoon, cream together the butter, shallots and dill until well combined. Stir in the lemon juice, cayenne and sea salt.

Using a sharp knife, lightly score the skinned side of the salmon on the diagonal. Cut the salmon crosswise into 4 equal pieces. Dry the top of each slice with paper towels, then spread with the dill and shallot butter. Place the salmon skin side down on the bed of heated salt and cover with a tight-fitting lid. If the cast-iron skillet has a pouring lip, plug it with a piece of aluminum foil. Cook the salmon over medium-high heat for 30 to 40 minutes, or until the salmon is opaque and slightly firm.

Remove the lid and, using a wide spatula, carefully remove the salmon to 4 warmed plates. Garnish each serving with a lemon wedge and dill sprigs or flowers. Serve immediately. *Serves 4*

Sautéed Shrimp with Cilantro and Parsley Sauce

For a festive Latin presentation, serve these tangy shrimps on a bed of colorful lettuces such as red and green oakleaf, Lollo Rossa, frisée and romaine—the colors of the Mexican flag.

Cilantro and Parsley Sauce:
3 tablespoons finely chopped fresh cilantro
1 tablespoon finely chopped fresh parsley
1 clove garlic, minced
1 tablespoon thinly sliced green onion top
1 fresh jalapeño chili pepper, seeded and finely chopped
1/2 teaspoon salt
1/4 cup peanut oil

2 tablespoons unsalted butter
2 tablespoons peanut oil
2 pounds large shrimp (approximately 48), peeled and deveined
3 tablespoons freshly squeezed lemon juice
Salt and freshly ground pepper, to taste

To make the sauce, in a medium bowl, whisk together all the ingredients until well blended. Set aside.

In a large sauté pan over medium heat, melt the butter with the peanut oil. When the bubbles have subsided, add the shrimp and sauté until they just begin to turn pink. Add the lemon juice and salt and pepper. Sauté for 3 to 4 minutes more, or until just opaque. Add the reserved cilantro and parsley sauce and quickly toss the shrimp until they are well coated.

Divide the shrimp among 4 warmed plates. Serve immediately. *Serves 4*

Herbs and Spices Crab Boil

In Louisiana parlance, a boil is the mixture of herbs and spices added to stock for cooking crab —or crawfish or shrimp—for a zesty feast. In this recipe, dried herbs, preferably garden grown and home dried, play a major role, along with an assortment of spicy seeds.

Herbs and Spices Boil:
2 teaspoons dried sweet basil
1 teaspoon dried sweet marjoram
1 teaspoon dried thyme
1/2 teaspoon dried chives
3 dried bay laurel leaves, coarsely chopped
1 dried Tabasco or cayenne chili pepper, stemmed and coarsely chopped
1/4 cup coriander seeds
1/4 cup mustard seeds
2 tablespoons ground allspice
2 tablespoons celery seeds
2 tablespoons dill seeds
1 tablespoon ground cloves

8 quarts water
2 tablespoons salt
2 lemons, sliced
2 stalks celery, plus the small, light green inner heart with leaves attached
1 yellow onion, sliced
4 to 4 1/2 pounds live crabs

To prepare the herbs and spices boil, combine all the ingredients in a large bowl. With the tips of your fingers, lightly crumble the herb leaves and stir to mix well with other ingredients. Place the mixture on a double layer of cheese-cloth. Bring the corners together to form a pouch and tie securely with kitchen string.

In a 10- to 12-quart enameled kettle, combine the water, salt, lemons, celery, onion and cheese-cloth pouch. Bring to a boil over high heat. Reduce the heat to medium, cover and simmer for 20 minutes.

Uncover, raise the heat to high and bring to a rolling boil. Add the crabs and boil briskly for 10 to 15 minutes, or until the shells turn bright red. Turn off the heat and allow the crabs to remain in the water for 10 minutes.

Remove the crabs with tongs and discard the cooking liquid. When cool enough to handle, crack the crabs and pile them on a large serving platter. Serve hot or cold. *Serves 4 to 6*

Bay Scallops Poached in Wine with Mushrooms and Thyme

*Plump bay scallops are wonderfully sweet and marry well with thyme, whose tiny leaves
are also pungently sweet. Serve the same wine at the table as you use for cooking the scallops.*

1 pound fresh crimini or white mushrooms
2 tablespoons salted butter
1/4 cup finely chopped shallots
*2 small carrots, cut into julienne strips 2 1/2 inches
   long and 1/4 inch wide*

*1 tablespoon plus 2 teaspoons finely chopped
   fresh thyme*
Salt and freshly ground black pepper, to taste
1 cup Sauvignon Blanc or other dry white wine
2 pounds bay scallops
1 tablespoon finely chopped fresh curly-leaf parsley

Preheat the oven to 150 degrees F.

Remove the stems from the mushrooms and save them for another purpose. Cut the caps into thin slices.

In a large skillet over medium heat, melt the butter. Add the mushrooms, shallots, carrots, 1 tablespoon thyme, salt and pepper and stir together well. Cover and cook over low heat for 10 minutes, or until the carrots are tender.

Add the wine and bring to a boil. Reduce the heat to medium, cover and simmer for 2 minutes. Uncover, add the scallops and stir to combine. Raise the heat to medium–high, re-cover and cook for approximately 5 minutes, or until the scallops have turned opaque and are springy to the touch. Take care not to overcook.

Using a slotted spoon, transfer the scallops, mushrooms, shallots and carrots to a warmed platter. Sprinkle with the remaining 2 teaspoons thyme and toss quickly to combine. Place in the warm oven with the door ajar and reserve.

Raise the heat to high and reduce the pan juices to approximately 2/3 cup. Pour the pan juices over the scallops and sprinkle with the parsley. Serve immediately. *Serves 4*

BEVERAGES

Herbs perfume some of our classic beverages: a mint julep in an iced silver cup; hot Christmas punch spiked with rosemary; a traditional woodruff-scented Maibowle.

Herb teas, or *tisanes,* are a favorite of the French. They know that a cup sipped directly after a meal is an excellent digestive, or that when taken just before bedtime, it will lull the drinker to sleep. Apple-scented chamomile in dried sachets is a French tradition at afternoon or evening teas.

In Early American stillrooms, housewives used mint to temper a beverage heady with an overabundance of brandy. An iced tea flavored with spearmint and a dash of fresh strawberry juice cools one down without the generous measure of brandy.

The French cherish their eaux-de-vie, cordials, liqueurs and refreshing herb- and fruit-flavored wines, too. Italians love their peach Bellinis and fruit-flavored grappas, and Russians relish their vodkas flavored with lemon or orange peels, cherries or herbs. With a garden of herbs nearby, a delicate licorice-scented vodka made with fresh tarragon sprigs can be ready to drink in a day. A mimosa is the classic brunch beverage of orange juice and Champagne. By slipping in a muddle of mint, it is transformed into a pale green sparkling beverage.

Peppermint Mimosa

*At the height of summer, when
the plantation of mint in the garden perfumes
the air, it's time to use fresh peppermint to
flavor your brunch-time mimosas.*

6 tablespoons finely chopped fresh peppermint leaves,
   plus fresh peppermint sprigs, for garnish
1/4 cup granulated sugar
1 cup strained freshly squeezed orange juice
3 bottles high-quality Champagne, well chilled

In a small ceramic bowl, combine the chopped
peppermint and sugar. Using a wooden pestle,
crush the leaves until a paste is formed. Add the
orange juice and mix well. Spoon the mixture
into a fine-mesh sieve placed over a bowl and
press against the mint paste to extract the juice.

Pour 2 tablespoons of the strained juice
into each of 8 chilled 8-ounce Champagne
glasses. Carefully fill with Champagne. Garnish
each glass with sprig of peppermint and serve
immediately. *Serves 8*

Tarragon-Flavored Vodka

*Herb-flavored vodkas are Old World
favorites called "little rays of sunshine." Served icy
cold in thimble-sized liqueur glasses, they are
an elegant and unique beverage to accompany
smoked salmon, trout or other smoked fish or caviar.
Tarragon flavors vodka with a delicate anise
bouquet. Spearmint, peppermint or lavender can
also be used to scent quality vodkas.*

Two 4-inch-long sprigs of fresh tarragon
One 375-ml bottle imported 80 proof vodka

Rinse and thoroughly dry the tarragon with
paper towels. Place the sprigs in the bottle of
vodka, cover and allow the flavors to infuse at
room temperature for 24 hours. Taste to deter-
mine if the vodka is sufficiently flavored with
the tarragon. If not, allow the vodka to sit for
another 24 hours, or until the flavor is strong
enough to suit your taste.

Remove and discard the tarragon sprigs.
Store the bottle in the freezer. The vodka will
not freeze, but it will become syrupy, which
is the proper consistency for serving. To
serve, pour into 1-ounce liqueur glasses. *Makes
1 1/2 cups; serves 12*

Herb Teas

Because of Peter Rabbit and his run-in with Farmer MacGregor, chamomile is the herb most associated with a tea believed to calm your nerves. It is true that apple-scented chamomile tea makes a tranquilizing herbal nightcap, but it also makes a pleasant afternoon pick-me-up brewed with a refreshing sprig of mint.

After the Boston Tea Party, when all the black tea available was floating in the harbor, the colonists turned to herbal teas, promptly naming them liberty teas. They brewed them from rosemary, lavender, thyme, sage, mint and lemon balm. You can repeat history by drinking these delightful brews.

Also known by the French term *tisane,* herb teas do not darken perceptibly as they steep, so their strength must be gauged by taste rather than sight. To make an herb tea, use 1 tablespoon fresh herbs or 1 teaspoon dried herbs for each cup of boiling water. Rinse the teapot with boiling water and then add the herbs to it. Pour boiling water over the herbs and allow them to steep for 3 to 5 minutes. Strain and serve.

Tasty additions to herb teas include honey or brown cane sugar crystals and the juice of lemons, limes, oranges, strawberries or other fruits. Brandy, gin or liqueurs give teas a punch. Spices such as coriander, ginger, caraway, fennel, cinnamon, cardamom or vanilla can be added to both hot and iced teas to create sensational teatime drinks.

Chamomile Tisane

The flowers of both the annual German chamomile and the perennial Roman chamomile can be used to make this delicate and soothing apple-scented tisane. The German variety, however, has the flavor edge. A sliced apple adds a soupçon of flavor that compounds the apple taste of the herb blossoms. This mild tea is perfect served with buttery madeleines.

2 tablespoons fresh chamomile flowers
2 cups boiling water
2 thin slices of Red Delicious apple

Honey or brown cane sugar crystals, to taste (optional)
2 thin, crescent-shaped slices Red Delicious apple,
*   for garnish (optional)*

Rinse the chamomile flowers with cool water. Rinse a small ceramic teapot with boiling water. Add the thin apple slices to the pot and mash them with a wooden pestle.

Add the chamomile flowers to the pot and pour in the boiling water. Cover and let steep for 3 to 5 minutes, or until the flavor suits you.

Strain into 2 warmed cups. If desired, add honey or sugar and garnish each serving with a crescent-shaped apple slice. *Serves 2*

Left to right: Iced Spearmint Tea with Strawberry Nectar and French Lavender Lemonade (recipe p. 90)
with Artist's Palette Herb Flower Canapés (recipe p. 31)

Iced Spearmint Tea with Strawberry Nectar

All the mints make refreshing iced teas. Fortunately, it is easy to have a large supply of all kinds of fresh and dried mint on hand, as all the varieties grow exuberantly. Strawberries color this spearmint tea crimson, but the cool green taste of the herb comes through. To compensate for the melting ice, make an extra 2 cups of the tea and freeze them in an ice-cube tray. Tea iced with the cubes will remain as strong as when first poured.

Sugar Syrup:
1 cup granulated sugar
1 cup water
Zest of 1 orange, cut into strips

4 1/2 cups water
1/4 cup dried spearmint, or 3/4 cup fresh spearmint

1 cup sliced strawberries
1 cup strained freshly squeezed orange juice
Ice cubes
Fresh spearmint sprigs and strawberry slices,
*   for garnish (optional)*

To make the sugar syrup, in a medium saucepan, combine the sugar, water and orange zest. Bring to a boil, stirring to dissolve the sugar. Remove from the heat and let cool. Pour the syrup through a fine-mesh sieve placed over a bowl, pressing down on the orange zest with the back of a spoon to extract as much of the flavorful oils as possible. Discard the zest and set the syrup aside.

In a medium saucepan, bring the water to a boil, then remove from the heat. Crumble the spearmint and add to the water; let steep for 5 minutes to obtain a strong infusion. Strain through a fine-mesh sieve placed over a large bowl. Discard the mint and let the infusion cool.

Meanwhile, place the strawberries in a fine-mesh sieve set over a medium bowl. With the back of a spoon, press the berries through the sieve, leaving the pulp and seeds behind. Scrape any purée clinging to the bottom of the sieve, and then add all the purée to the cooled infusion.

Add the orange juice and 1/2 cup of the sugar syrup to the tea and stir vigorously. Taste and add more sugar syrup as desired. (Store any remaining sugar syrup in the refrigerator for when you make another batch of tea.) Cover and refrigerate the tea until well chilled.

Just before serving, fill a large pitcher with ice and add the tea. Pour into chilled glasses. Garnish with a sprig of mint and a slice of strawberry, if desired. *Serves 6*

French Lavender Lemonade

This refreshing rosy-colored lemonade is perfumed with just a hint of the sweetness and floral scent of French lavender.

Lavender Infusion:
2 1/2 cups water
1 1/2 cups granulated sugar
1/4 cup fresh French lavender leaves, coarsely
    chopped

2 1/2 cups water
1 cup strained freshly squeezed lemon juice
Granulated sugar, to taste
Ice cubes
6 to 8 sprigs of fresh lavender, for garnish

To make the lavender infusion, combine the water and sugar in a medium saucepan. Bring the water to a boil, stirring to dissolve the sugar. Add the lavender and remove from the heat. Cover and let the infusion cool to room temperature. Strain and discard the lavender.

Pour the infusion into a glass pitcher and add the water and lemon juice. Stir well, adding additional sugar if desired. Refrigerate until chilled. Just before serving, stir the lemonade again and fill the pitcher with ice. Pour into chilled glasses and garnish each serving with a sprig of lavender. *Serves 6 to 8*

METRIC CONVERSIONS

Liquid Weights

U.S. Measurements	Metric Equivalents
1/4 teaspoon	1.23 ml
1/2 teaspoon	2.5 ml
3/4 teaspoon	3.7 ml
1 teaspoon	5 ml
1 dessertspoon	10 ml
1 tablespoon (3 teaspoons)	15 ml
2 tablespoons (1 ounce)	30 ml
1/4 cup	60 ml
1/3 cup	80 ml
1/2 cup	120 ml
2/3 cup	160 ml
3/4 cup	180 ml
1 cup (8 ounces)	240 ml
2 cups (1 pint)	480 ml
3 cups	720 ml
4 cups (1 quart)	1 litre
4 quarts (1 gallon)	3 3/4 litres

Dry Weights

U.S. Measurements	Metric Equivalents
1/4 ounce	7 grams
1/3 ounce	10 grams
1/2 ounce	14 grams
1 ounce	28 grams
1 1/2 ounces	42 grams
1 3/4 ounces	50 grams
2 ounces	57 grams
3 ounces	85 grams
3 1/2 ounces	100 grams
4 ounces (1/4 pound)	114 grams
6 ounces	170 grams
8 ounces (1/2 pound)	227 grams
9 ounces	250 grams
16 ounces (1 pound)	464 grams

Temperatures

Fahrenheit	Celsius (Centigrade)
32°F (water freezes)	0°C
200°F	95°C
212°F (water boils)	100°C
250°F	120°C
275°F	135°C
300°F (slow oven)	150°C
325°F	160°C
350°F (moderate oven)	175°C
375°F	190°C
400°F (hot oven)	205°C
425°F	220°C
450°F (very hot oven)	230°C
475°F	245°C
500°F (extremely hot oven)	260°C

Length

U.S. Measurements	Metric Equivalents
1/8 inch	3 mm
1/4 inch	6 mm
3/8 inch	1 cm
1/2 inch	1.2 cm
3/4 inch	2 cm
1 inch	2.5 cm
1 1/4 inches	3.1 cm
1 1/2 inches	3.7 cm
2 inches	5 cm
3 inches	7.5 cm
4 inches	10 cm
5 inches	12.5 cm

Approximate Equivalents

1 kilo is slightly more than 2 pounds
1 litre is slightly more than 1 quart
1 meter is slightly over 3 feet
1 centimeter is approximately 3/8 inch

INDEX